LATINA SELF-PORTRAITS

UNIVERSITY OF NEW MEXICO PRESS *Albuquerque*

BRIDGET KEVANE & JUANITA HEREDIA

LATINA
Self-Portraits

Interviews
with
Contemporary
Women Writers

©2000 by the University of New Mexico Press
All rights reserved.
First edition
Library of Congress Cataloging-in-Publication Data
Kevane, Bridget A., 1963–
    Latina self-portraits : interviews with contemporary women writers /
Bridget Kevane and Juanita Heredia.—1st ed.
        p.   cm.
Includes bibliographical references.
    ISBN 0-8263-1971-8 (alk. paper)—ISBN 0-8263-1972-6 (pbk. : alk. paper)
1. American literature—Hispanic American authors—History and
criticism—Theory, etc.   2. American literature—Women authors—
History and criticism—Theory, etc.   3. American literature—20th
century—History and criticism—Theory, etc.   4. Women authors,
American—20th century—Interviews.   5. Hispanic American women—
Intellectual life.   6. Hispanic American women—Interviews.   7. Hispanic
Americans in literature.   I. Heredia, Juanita, 1966–   II. Title.
    PS153.H56 K48 2000
    810.9'9287'08968—dc21   99-050785

Contents

ACKNOWLEDGMENTS   vii

INTRODUCTION
Perennial Travelers:
   The Forging of Latina Literature   I
Critical Matters:
   Defining the Literary Space of Latina Literature   10

1 CITIZEN OF THE WORLD
   An Interview with Julia Alvarez   19

2 THE SPIRIT OF HUMOR
   An Interview with Denise Chávez   33

3 A HOME IN THE HEART
   An Interview with Sandra Cisneros   45

4 A SIDE VIEW
   An Interview with Rosario Ferré   59

5   AT HOME ON THE PAGE
    An Interview with Cristina García   69

6   PA'LANTE
    An Interview with Nicholasa Mohr   83

7   CITY OF DESIRE
    An Interview with Cherríe Moraga   97

8   THE POETIC TRUTH
    An Interview with Judith Ortiz Cofer   109

9   A PUERTO RICAN EXISTENTIALIST IN BROOKLYN
    An Interview with Esmeralda Santiago   125

10 PRAYING FOR KNOWLEDGE
    An Interview with Helena María Viramontes   141

    BIBLIOGRAPHY   155

Acknowledgments

Bridget Kevane wishes to express her heartfelt thanks to the following colleagues for their generous comments, suggestions, and support throughout the project: Héctor Calderón for offering initial inspiration, encouragement, and criticism; Jack Jelinski for the intellectual generosity and time he spent with me on developing many ideas in the book; and Charles Baraw for all the lively conversations about Chicana/Latina literature. I am also grateful to Dean James McMillan of the College of Letters and Science at MSU for funding part of the telephone interviews and transcription and travel to Puerto Rico. Finally, I am eternally grateful to my family: my parents, brothers, and sisters who support everything I do, and my husband and daughter who endured the ups and downs of this project with love and patience.

Juanita Heredia wishes to thank many colleagues and friends who have contributed to the making of this book. I am grateful for their encouragement and support, especially during moments of time constraints and unforeseen obstacles. I am particularly thankful to my colleague Héctor Calderón, who read this manuscript from beginning to end and helped develop my critical thinking on Chicana Latina literature. I also wish to thank my colleagues, Barbara Curiel, Lisbeth Gant-Britton, Erlinda Gonzales-Berry, and Leticia Hernández-Linares, for their insights and challenging ideas about Chicana/Latina literature and criticism. I am also eternally indebted to my friends, Nerissa De Jesus, Sally Hui, I-Lin Kuo, Linda Mirelez, Andrew Mulholland, and Alex Quintanilla for their time and patience in the forging of this book. It goes without saying that my parents, Felix and Julia Heredia, provided understanding and wisdom during this period as did my brother Felix Z. Heredia.

Both of us wish to thank our editors, Andrea Otañez and Barbara Guth for their support, skill, and enthusiasm; and Tracy Hawke for all her administrative help. This book of interviews could not have been possible without the collaboration and generosity of our ten writers, Julia Alvarez, Denise Chávez, Sandra Cisneros, Rosario Ferré, Cristina García, Nicholasa Mohr, Cherríe Moraga, Judith Ortiz Cofer, Esmeralda Santiago, and Helena María Viramontes. We are grateful to Susan Bergholz for allowing us the opportunity to speak with her writers.

Introduction

PERENNIAL TRAVELERS: THE FORGING OF LATINA LITERATURE:

Historical Overview:

An important phenomenon is occurring in American cultural and literary studies. Latina voices are attaining a prominence in American letters that shows the growing diversity of the discourse on culture and the arts in the United States. It is now clear that U.S. literature has substantial and significant roots that reach beyond U.S. borders. The American story is one that is increasingly being told by women from a hemispheric rather than a single national perspective. This book illustrates the growth of a contemporary Latina literary tradition that now spans thirty years.

This collection of interviews with ten prominent Latina writers is the first of its kind. We have selected this form to explore the authors' cultural backgrounds and relevant personal histories that may not always be found in "strictly" academic criticism. There is a need for an alternative form of criticism that is both personal and pedagogical, analytic and reflective. Therefore, we asked questions that allowed the authors to reflect on culture, history, gender, and the arts in general. By speaking one on one, we uncovered issues that preoccupied them as women, as "translators" of culture and history. As the first generation to cross directly between two cultures, they can describe firsthand the experience of being at the interstices of two worlds. These Latina writers can serve as models to younger generations because they have succeeded in being recognized as artists and as women despite all the odds against them in U.S. society.

We must also understand the process and history behind their achievements, another factor that is overlooked in contemporary criticism. In these interviews the authors share revealing qualities of their humanity that often elude capture by critical discourse, qualities that are only alluded to in their literary works. As each author speaks of her experiences, she lays out a personal cartography for others to follow in the solitary voyage of writing in modern times. This collection photographs these moments in their lives by transforming an oral narrative into a written, permanent history, a new way of making criticism.

Julia Alvarez, Denise Chávez, Sandra Cisneros, Rosario Ferré, Cristina García, Nicholasa Mohr, Cherríe Moraga, Judith Ortiz Cofer, Esmeralda Santiago, and Helena María Viramontes represent a broad spectrum of Latina literature. Composed of Chicana, Cuban, Dominican, Puerto Rican, and other writers who descend from a combined U.S.–Latin American heritage, Latina literature is finally receiving national attention in the 1990s. In her groundbreaking essay, "On Finding a Latino Voice," Julia Alvarez has described this movement as a literary made-in-the-USA boom, a recognition based on critical and commercial success. Although this movement consists of writers who may be described generically as "Latina," they are not a homogeneous group but instead reflect a diversity of origins. What is certain is that each writer has roots in more than one culture, that each is a hybrid. Migrations of Latinos in the United States have affected the formation of each artist included in this book. For example, each Chicana writer associates differently with Mexican culture. One is from Chicago, another is from Las Cruces, New Mexico, and others are from Los Angeles. Even though these writers were born and educated in the United States, they have a connection with Mexico through childhood and adult travels, family stories, or the invention of an imaginary homeland. Their conversations demonstrate how Mexico embodies an integral component of culture and triggers memories of ancestors and their untold stories. The Latina Caribbean patterns of movement play a role in their history as well. As part of a diaspora, the Puerto Rican writers we interviewed have lived in Brooklyn, New Jersey, Spanish Harlem, and Ponce. They have undergone the "p'aquí and p'allá" phenomenon of traveling back and forth between the mainland and the island at various stages of their lives. Each writer identifies with Puerto Rico differently. The Cuban and Dominican writers, all of them daughters of exiled communities, could not return to their homelands until they were adults. Without the possibility of return, they learned about their cultures through family stories, memory, and imagination, the latter especially if they did not grow up in a Latino environment in the United States. Although this group of bicultural and bilingual women writers may appear to constitute a recent voice in American literature, this community has emerged from a complex and varied history.

The writers in this collection reflect dramatic shifts in recent political history. The Cuban Revolution of 1959 and the Trujillo dictatorship in the Dominican Republic produced a generation of exiles who migrated from their homeland to the United States. People of Mexican and Caribbean descent, both immigrants and citizens, became a visible part of American social and political life in the 1960s. Through the Chicano, civil rights, Puerto Rican, and women's movements, Latinas made inroads into American society. Because of the social activism and institutional reforms that were an outgrowth of these movements, Latinas gained access to an educational system that enabled them to develop careers as writers and academics. These social movements in the Northern Hemisphere transformed the demographics of Latino communities in the United States, particularly in the East, Midwest, and Southwest. If it were not for the social movements of the 1960s, it is doubtful whether U.S. Latina literature would exist today.

While the historical context of Latina literature provides a background for understanding these writers as a group, a collective voice, it is also necessary to look at each writer as an individual to appreciate her own development as an artist. By examining the collective and the individual, we can better comprehend how Latina literature has established itself as a legitimate field of study and as an art form with popular appeal.

Nicholasa Mohr was one of the first contemporary Latina writers to publish a novel, *Nilda* (1973), a coming-of-age story of a Puerto Rican adolescent in Spanish Harlem during World War II. In the 1980s Chicana writers experienced a literary movement of their own. Cherríe Moraga coedited literary anthologies, *This Bridge Called My Back: Writings by Radical Women of Color* (1981) and *Cuentos: Stories by Latinas* (1983), that also included work by Latína lesbian writers. Sandra Cisneros's first work of prose fiction, *The House on Mango Street* (1984), deals with the early years of a Mexican-American girl in a Chicano/Latino neighborhood in the 1960s in Chicago. Helena María Viramontes published *The Moths and Other Stories* (1985), which represents the urban community of East Los Angeles in the 1960s and 1970s through female experiences. Denise Chávez's collection of short stories, *The Last of the Menu Girls* (1986), portrays the lives of families in New Mexico through the eyes of a female adolescent. These five works illustrate the differences in communities that exist in Chicano culture and expand the portrayal of Chicana experience in literature by showing a broad range—adult and adolescent, rural and urban—as well as the various degrees of contact with mainstream and other ethnic groups. At the same time, Judith Ortiz Cofer's memoir, *Silent Dancing: A Partial Remembrance of a Puerto Rican Childhood* (1989), records a female adolescent's growing-up experiences in New Jersey and on the island in the 1960s. By the end of the 1980s, the academic community, scholars, critics, and universities, began to recognize Latina literature's institutional value and the public its literary merits. In fact, the first critical anthology that introduces Latina literature, *Breaking Boundaries: Latina Writings and Critical Readings* (1989), initiated a dialogue among writers, critics, and the public at large.

When I was an undergraduate at the University of California at Berkeley in 1989, little did I realize that I was witnessing the institutionalization of Chicana/Latina literature. Cherríe Moraga, a beginning playwright and virtually unknown at the time, visited our class on Chicana writers as a guest speaker. Needless to say, Moraga's presence captured the students' attention because she was able to speak about herself and the writing process. This was an illuminating approach to teaching literature: it was personal and pedagogical (which coincides with our aim here). The encouragement of professors, mostly Chicanas and Latinas, would bring about gradual changes at universities across the United States and contribute to the emergence of a Latina literary movement. What is remarkable about Latina literature is that it transcends disciplinary boundaries. Although most works of Latina fiction are primarily written in English, the incorporation of Spanish and the engagement with Latino cultures both inside the United States and beyond its borders make it relevant to many disciplines: cultural studies, gender studies, Latino/a studies, Chicano/a studies, Caribbean studies, American studies, Latin American studies, and English and Spanish literature departments. The wave of Latina writing that took shape in the 1980s would bring about a historical moment in the following decade in American letters for women writers in the borderlands.

By the 1990s Latina literature had reached a milestone in production and national reception as the Latino community expanded to include more cultural groups in the United States and the Caribbean. Ferré explains, "A new literary boom vox is playing in the Caribbean that is very audible in the United States today." This decade is also significant in that Latina writers are receiving recognition for a variety of literary forms—criticism, prose, poetry, and theater—in literary reviews, academic journals, and conferences from an increasingly wider U.S. critical community. Judith Ortiz Cofer's *The Line of the Sun* (1990) provides further insight into U.S.–Puerto Rican relations through family migrations. Julia Alvarez's novel *How the García Girls Lost Their Accents* (1991) chronicles a Dominican family's exile in the United States, and Sandra Cisneros's *Woman Hollering Creek and Other Stories* (1991) explores the complex relationship between Chicanos and Mexicans on both sides of the international border. Cristina García, a Cuban writer raised and educated in the United States, portrays the experiences of a family in exile after the Cuban Revolution in *Dreaming in Cuban* (1992). Esmeralda Santiago offers another perspective on the Puerto Rican diaspora with her autobiography, *When I Was Puerto Rican* (1993). Moraga's *The Last Generation* (1993) addresses the effects of losing one's culture in U.S. society. Denise Chávez's *Face of an Angel* (1994) explores the trials and tribulations of Chicano culture and gender through a waitress's perspective. Helena María Viramontes's *Under the Feet of Jesus* (1995) captures the survival of a migrant family working in the orchards of California. Although she had been writing since the 1970s in Spanish, Rosario Ferré crossed into the English language with the publication of her historical novel, *The House on the Lagoon* (1995), in which she presents the history of Puerto Rican society on the island. Although Latina writers may write in other genres, the decade of the 1990s is evidently the boom in Latina prose fiction as the 1960s were for the Latin American novel. These Latina writers from different generations have contributed to the installation of Latina prose fiction in the American literary canon. In fact, schools and colleges across the United States have begun to adopt some of these works as required reading.

A Question of Gender

Another purpose of this book is to show how Latina writers are broadening present American literary feminism by telling stories of disempowered people, particularly women, on both sides of the U.S.–Latin American border. By representing images and experiences that challenge patriarchy and the dominant American society, Latina literature is undoubtedly transforming U.S. literature. Through the creation of complex characters in Latina literature, the writers demonstrate the evolution of a culture and its impact on society. At the same time their efforts serve as an ode to the spirit of perseverance, strength, and wisdom in women who may be overlooked in society. The writers in this collection discuss how they reenvision history through fiction, myths, and stories of their own.

By reconfiguring the past, Latina writers offer a different perspective of Latina female characters in literary history. For example, Cisneros's and Moraga's fiction is deeply committed to redefining the image of Malinche, the Aztec indigenous woman who was a translator for Hernán Córtes, by humanizing her, as the feminist critic Norma Alarcón suggests, by "putting flesh back on the object." Viramontes uses Spanish colonial Mexico and the experiences of East Los Angeles as a point of departure in her novel, *They Came with Their Dogs*, to show the effects of violence on colonized people. Chávez is concerned with the impact of Mexican cinema, the images and symbols of romantic lovers, on a generation of women in *Loving Pedro Infante*. Ferré examines the role of women in Puerto Rican history from the independence period to contemporary times in *The House on the Lagoon*. Cofer carefully reconstructs the period of the 1950s in Puerto Rico to show a changing society and its effects on women in her novel *In the Line of the Sun*. *In the Time of the Butterflies*, Alvarez looks at the effects of a dictatorship on four sisters in an underground movement in the 1960s in the Dominican Republic through myths and legends. When the writers decide to represent unrecognized females in literary history, Latina literature is not only recovering the past and making it come alive, it is also examining it for the future. Viramontes captures the spirit of the women unacknowledged in history when she says, "Just when I think I'm sinking into hopelessness, I begin to think . . . about the stories of the mujeres out there, their sheer arrogance to survive, their incredible strength to take care of others, and the brutalities that continue to exist, and then I become inspired and I am no longer afraid of confronting and sitting with these companions [of loneliness], like 'Okay, Lucha Libre, let's get rolling.'" The significance of these authors lies in how they transform female characters in literature to offer an understanding of their survival in a more humane society.

The writers in this collection also comment on their relationships with their mothers, who may be separated from them by culture, education, ideology, or sexual orientation. Alvarez, Cisneros, Cofer, Ferré, García, Mohr, and Viramontes, for example, speak about intense relationships between mothers and daughters, which offer them a lens through which to understand themselves as women from a different generation and culture. On the one hand, the daughters are grateful for their mothers' efforts in motivating them to pursue their goals. On the other hand, they are often critical of the older generation and, by extension, of the culture that shaped their mothers. In this sense the interviews provide insight into how Latina mother/daughter relationships have played a key role in the writers' lives. Cisneros says of her mother, "She has helped me create Latina characters who are very antistereotypical. I get so tired of seeing these religious fanatics. My mother is very anti-Catholic. She is a freethinker, very bright, an amazing and extraordinary Latina woman." Qualities such as these have unquestionably led the writers to the freedom to create, to explore prohibited terrain, and essentially to develop a feminist consciousness of what it means to be a Latina writer in the United States. How does a Latina writer reconcile the commitments to the culture that bred her with her own ambitions and goals? These writers are not just questioning values but actually redefining what womanhood, sexuality, spirituality, and community mean to them as daughters of a mixed U.S.–Latin American heritage. By offering a variety of opinions on the issue of gender, these writers also attest to the multifaceted nature of the Latina experience: each writer takes an individual road to define her own kind of Latina feminism. Moreover, as these writers have become strong and independent thinkers, they have made an impact on the perception of Latinas in the United States. The collective voice of Latina women is bringing about a new perspective in American culture— one that takes into account a diversity of experience.

With a growing awareness of globalization, Latina writers join hands with women writers from other cultures who also seek to belong to a wider community beyond their cultural boundaries. The women in this collection refer to their alliances with Catalan, Haitian, and Latin American as well as African-American, Asian-American, and Native American women writers. This brand of sisterhood is one that transcends cultural boundaries to connect with others on a transnational level.

Translating Stories, Making Form

Stories alone, however, do not make the artist. The interviews in this book also reveal how each writer is preoccupied with finding the proper form for the content of her stories, thereby demonstrating the intricate relationship between style and subject matter. Language, whether poetic or colloquial, allows the artist to present stories that reflect her imagination and personal experiences. As each writer in this book has been involved in translating stories from one culture to another, in the process she has also been engaged in making a form of her own.

It is noteworthy that Latina literature has been influenced by other arts. For example, Chávez's preparation as an actress informed the development of voice, character, dialogue, and even humor in her fiction. García's work as a journalist taught her to focus on the details in her fiction. Mohr learned how to handle imagery in her fiction through her training in the graphic arts. Santiago's essay writing enabled her to construct her fiction more carefully. Viramontes's screenwriting helped her to hone the imagery in her first novel. The arts complement one another. As Cisneros advises writers, "I would encourage them to read everything, even other genres that they are not writing in. I would tell them to become very familiar with the other arts—painting, music—all the arts teach each other."

All the writers we interviewed agree on one common technique that is shaping the form of contemporary Latina literature: storytelling. This oral tradition, inherited from mothers, fathers, and grandparents, is foundational in Latina literature, an element specifically tied to cultural heritage. Being bilingual and bicultural, these writers are translators of oral stories, often told to them in Spanish. Like the African-American, Asian-American, and Native American traditions, the Latina tradition celebrates this oral quality as a means to engage in a dialogue with the antepasados, with those who have gone before. By preserving the stories of their ancestors, the writers are able to re-create the past to envision a more hopeful future. Alvarez pays homage to the women in her family in the

Dominican Republic for telling her stories that she employs in her fiction. Chávez also incorporates the stories of the women in her family in her work. Cisneros pays tribute to her mother for the "working-class Chicago voice" in her writing. Cofer grew up in a matriarchal structure in Puerto Rico and uses her grandmother's "poetic truth" in her art. Mohr remembers how her mother told her the traditional Puerto Rican Juan Bobo stories, which now inform her own short stories. Moraga reserves a special place for her mamá for teaching her the art of story, which she feels explains her interest in theater. Cofer sums up storytelling's importance in culture and writing: "Storytelling is used in a culture to preserve its memories and to teach lessons for the same reason that artists write their stories. I give credit to the women in my family for giving me that lesson and some of the original stories that I used." This example gives validity to a technique that plays a role in the development of form in Latina literature: a personal apprenticeship that complements formal education.

Although Latina prose fiction has attained special prominence in the 1990s, many of the writers we interviewed discussed the importance of poetry. In the 1970s poetry was the dominant genre in Latina literature. Poets valued the use of the oral tradition, and most were able to recite and sing their lyrics to their respective communities. One only needs to look at the Chicano Renaissance or the Nuyorican café scene in the 1970s. Alvarez, Cisneros, Cofer, and Moraga began their literary careers as poets before venturing into the world of fiction. Their training in poetry helped to bring lyricism and concision to their prose. "Poetry is the best place to begin to write in any genre. It is about the condensed moment, the syntax of the palabra," explains Moraga.

In the 1980s and 1990s Latina writers employed many experimental techniques of modern fiction. For instance, they played with multiple perspectives, temporal fragmentation, and stream of consciousness, often enabling the reader to experience different levels of reality. Like other writers of modern literature, Latinas have reached another moment in form and language. Although it has not abandoned the storytelling technique in narrative, Latina literature also engages in a more stylized writing, more aware of figurative language. During this period the poetics has shifted more toward metaphors and symbols. For example, Cisneros infuses *The House on Mango Street* with elements of poetic symbolism, rhythm, rhyme, stream of consciousness, and figurative language. The self-consciousness of the protagonist also marks *The House on Mango Street* as a modern novel. Cisneros's use of the first person in the narrative also defines this work as a memoir. This work exemplifies how Latina fiction embraces a poetics that transcends the traditional boundaries of genre. By incorporating a combination of different styles, all these writers extend their modern works by combining formal aspects of prose writing with testimonial and personal experience. As Alvarez states. "Writers are often trying to work out their stories, the world according to how they were raised, the journey that they underwent, almost as if to clear the slate for other things that are coming." Clearly, the writers in this collection are not only telling their own stories but also translating the stories of others and making a form in the process.

As a scholar engaged in Chicana/Latina, American, and Latin American literary studies for more than a decade, I have seen this literary phenomenon developing as new voices continue to join the chorus. Chávez emphasizes, "What's so wonderful about Latino writers is that we are moving forward together, compañeros in la lucha de arte y literatura." What is exciting about these times is that all of us can participate in the growth of Latina literature as readers and respondents. This book aims to broaden the dialogue with artists, writers, and critics from various schools of thought. Latina literature will continue to reach a wider public who will read it for pleasure and for a deeper understanding of women writers at the borderlands of cultures.

Juanita Heredia

CRITICAL MATTERS:
DEFINING THE LITERARY SPACE OF LATINA LITERATURE

In the last decade there has been a wealth of criticism on Latina/Chicana writers that analyzes their work from diverse theoretical perspectives. Critical articles, books, and anthologies such as those cited in our bibliography have attempted to come to terms with Latina literature and to approach it from different angles—feminism, postmodernism, colonialism, and historicism, to name just a few. Yet there is little criticism on the craft of writing itself, on the formation of three generations of writers who have changed both the publishing and the academic world. A goal of this book was to invite the writers to discuss the craft of writing, what inspired them to become writers, and what they hoped to achieve. Within the context of that discussion, I wanted to hear what the writers had to say about the state of Latino literature, American literature, bilingualism, and their own experiences as women from Spanish-speaking backgrounds living in the United States. As a critic I believe a dialogue with the writers themselves can enlighten and challenge our thinking. And, in fact, I was challenged, provoked, and surprised by some of the issues discussed by the writers. This section of the introduction focuses on some of the many fascinating themes that emerged from the interviews.

As I scrutinized the interviews for commonalities and differences, I found myself drawn to how writing has transformed the lives of these women. Many did not start writing until late in life, after experiencing some life-changing event, like the birth of a child or a divorce. And many arrived at writing after full-time careers in journalism, graphic art, or motherhood. For these authors, writing has brought about a personal and public metamorphosis. When they write they are intimate poets seeking to understand their bicultural lives and the "professional" Latina writer, as García jokes. "Writing is the sanctity of grace," according to Chávez; a "meditation to the world," according to Viramontes. The page offers them a home, and language is the vehicle through which they can sort out their conflicting identities. Writing offers infinite possibilities of self-invention yet also the finite possibility of pinning the self down like a butterfly.

Aside from this personal meditation, however, the creative process contains another dimension—the ability to break the historical silence that has characterized their place in society as women, as Latinas, as childless Latinas, or as lesbian Latinas. Their writing is in part the result of a rage against the injustices these women have experienced or witnessed. Aware that their words have the power to speak to their community, to make a change, these writers have become intellectually responsible writers, conscious of speaking and writing for their community. This responsibility, in turn, has made the writers quite rigorous in their self-judgments. "I have to develop as a spiritual leader," says Cisneros, demanding of herself a wiser and better human being. When Viramontes realized she was writing about her community, she decided "to write the best that [she] could." This sense of responsibility presents a double bind, for though these writers have embraced their role and even dismissed the idea that they might sacrifice their art because of it, they are also criticized for it. On the one hand, critics and readers alike have become avid and passionate readers of Latina/Chicana literature. On the other hand, and perhaps because of the passionate response evoked by these works, unexpected demands are placed on these women; some say they are not representative enough of their ethnic communities, others complain that they are not good enough. I shall return to this again.

Like many writers, those interviewed in this book expressed a sense of regret about earlier work or said their work was not yet where they would like it to be. Moraga, perhaps the most forthright of all the women interviewed, said, "I feel like I haven't even begun to write the way that I want to write in my life." Cisneros wondered if perhaps she was naive in trying to capture all the voices of her community in some of her earlier work. Ferré sees her earlier works as exercises that have given her the stamina now to write novels. Mohr said that she had to accept all her work like one does one's children. They had a thing or two to say about literary critics as well. In fact, many of the writers see the work of critics as unproductive. However, the most surprising element in this discussion was that many of these writers, in the final editing of their interviews, eliminated comments on the role of the critic and literary criticism, comments that were revealing and insightful and honestly inquiring. Some said that literary criticism had become completely self-referential, that it was not read because it was not understood, that it served the critic's biases. Some complained of the sociological approach that has dominated the analysis; some criticized the idea of teaching only what is considered politically correct. The fact that most of the writers eliminated what could be perceived as controversial is telling. Sadly, it reflects a genuine lack of dialogue between writer and critic.

Still, the writers were not dismissive of literary criticism but wanted it to do more; perhaps provide a clearer sense of the place of Latina literature in the canon. With few exceptions, the writers see literary criticism as important. They appreciate it and see it as a critical component to the study and creation of literature. But the message in their comments is clear: Is the role of the critic to challenge the writer? Perhaps it is time for critics to address some fundamental questions that have been suggested from the interviews: What space does Latina literature occupy in the canon? How does it make its own unique contributions? Have issues of ethnicity displaced critical attention to the artistic value of Latina literature?

A Reciprocity of Influences

The current interest in the contribution of Latina/Chicana literature to the American literary canon is not unique. Many such redefinitions have taken place since the eighteenth century, and, in fact, American literature was at one time considered inferior to British literature. For a time Latin American literature suffered the same reception in Spanish departments. Although critics and writers would agree that Latino/a literature has expanded the canon, the definition of what it means to expand a literary tradition has been limited to concrete effects: the creation of centers dedicated to the study of Chicano, Cuban, and Puerto Rican culture across the nation since the 1960s and the inclusion of many of these writers on course syllabi. But with few exceptions, little work has been done to define how exactly this expansion has taken place. According to García, Latina literature has "muscled its way" into the canon. Viramontes says, "We are slowly having some bend." Alvarez says, "We are taken seriously now as American writers, not as writers of sociological interest only." Ferré says that Latina writers are synthesizing both cultures, the Hispanic and the Anglo, in "an effort to underline the importance of the 'side view' in them, of the border town." How has Latino literature bent the canon? How has the barrio muscled its way into the sonnet, for example?

The writers interviewed made it apparent that they have been shaped largely by the fruitful interaction of the American, European, and Latin American literary traditions. They have been inspired by Latin American writers such as Jorge Luis Borges, Gabriel García Márquez, and Juan Rulfo; American writers such as Emily Dickinson, William Faulkner, Flannery O'Connor, and Carson McCullers; and European writers such as Mercé Rodoreda, Federico García Lorca, and Jane Austen. To this rich mix they have added their bilingual, bicultural, Spanish-speaking heritage. But even though the writers have mentioned these influences time and again, the practice of examining influences has been neglected in the study of Latina literature. While critics assert these writers have expanded the canon, the actual relationship between them and previous canons needs more attention. Latina literatures are examined from all sorts of theoretical perspectives but not from within the very context of the literature that inspired them. Might this diminish their literature in some way, as lesser, sociological, gendered, or marginalized?

These writers first read within the canon. They borrowed from the canon, and it is worth examining what they return to it. Alvarez states that she is glad she read the canon: "I have to know *The Tempest* to fully understand *Calibán*." Ortiz Cofer finds that because she is aware of the mainstream and "not just limiting" herself to Latino studies, she can create more with her work. Some of these writers have said that a danger of knowing the canon, of course, is an initial desire to imitate the canonical voice, the voice of dead white men. The fortunate awareness that the canonical voice is not *their* voice represents a pivotal moment for these women. It marks a return to their roots, to their gender, their class, their homes. It is the spoken language of their home, the "Don't put so much vinegar in the lettuce" voice that Alvarez remembers or the "very tender, very sweet" diminutives of Mexican Spanish that Cisneros recalls.

The transition from canonical influence to individual creativity for the Latinas in this book is sometimes enhanced by reading other contemporary writers, another influence that has not been explored in depth. After finding their voice, many of these writers also made crucial discoveries in the works of Maxine Hong Kingston, Toni Morrison, or Gabriel García Márquez. The unparalleled license of the imagination in Márquez, or the negotiation between two different worlds in Kingston, liberated them to return to their roots through their literature.

This clear awareness of influences proves there is a layered richness to the works of these writers. There is a constant flux, a borrowing and returning from and to the canon. The sonnet is in the barrio in special ways. It is admired and then twisted or "exploded," as Alvarez says. The canon is in the barrio not only because most of these women have been educated within it but also because they admire it. Yet these writers claim an advantage by being on the outside. They are the trickster Calibán, or la Calibana, stealing from the master's tools.

Ofrendas al Canon

An obvious characteristic of Latina literature that makes it unique to the traditions that inspired it is the incorporation of Spanish both on a semantic and on a syntactic level. García thinks that "these new borderlands of languages is where it's happening." Spanglish, the combination of English and Spanish, characterizes these writers' private and public lives. Cisneros describes how the lyrical Spanish of her father and the working-class English of her mother contributed to her dual sense of language. Alvarez says that the English language, or the "wild horses of English," to use her term, contributed to her becoming a writer. Santiago uses Spanglish to communicate with her brothers and sisters because "it gets the job done." The combination of Spanish and English also plays a role in their creative work. Even their translations display a combination of languages. Ferré views her translations as "versions," whereas García went so far as to call the Spanish version of *The Agüero Sisters* a restoration, because the story actually takes place in Spanish. Many writers speak of the musicality, the cadence, and the rhythm that finds its way into their syntax. In Cisneros's "Eyes of Zapata" one is reading Spanish syntax in English. Cisneros admits that this story was a great challenge for her: "I had to create a voice that was totally different from any of the other voices that I created. This voice was set in a different historical time, which, one would understand from the syntax, was speaking Spanish."

The combination of English and Spanish has a very calculated use. Many choose not to italicize Spanish phrases or words anymore. Viramontes, Cofer, and García all said that their audience can pick up a "damn dictionary," to use García's phrase. Moraga finds the language important to her characters and to her work: "English has a very different rhythm, so when you choose that rhythm versus the softer, lyrical Spanish, it's totally calculated and wonderful." There are value words in Spanish that are untranslatable, like *dignidad*, which responds to certain poetic meanings that do not quite hold in English and, most important, do not maintain the cultural integrity of their characters. Spanglish is communication, language, poetry. Each writer, when asked, categorically denied that Spanglish is tainting either language, Spanish or English. Latina literature has returned to the canon a truly bilingual American literature. A sprinkling of words has evolved into full paragraphs in Spanish. The writers are demanding that their readers acknowledge the Spanish and that they acknowledge that Spanish has become part of the American landscape. The ultimate consequences of this linguistic uniqueness remain to be seen. The bilingual literature may be accepted as a part of the canon, or it may contribute to the unfortunate perception that Latina literature is not mainstream literature.

La Crítica

Another issue that will bear on the ultimate definition of Latina literature is the bête noir of its ethnicity. Nowhere is this more clearly illustrated than in the dispute ignited by Ilan Stavans in the *Chronicle of Higher Education* (January 1998). Stavans's comments to the effect that Latino literature is immature, among other things, were exaggerated, to say the least. But the response to his comments was equally devoid of critical scope. Stavans was accused of not understanding Chicano literature because he is not Chicano. Further, he was criticized for asking that critics set aside the "ethnic pride" that is blindly dominating this literature. The request to set aside ethnic restrictions might open doors to a more productive dialogue. In our interviews all the writers recoiled from this embattled arena where political ethnicity has monopolized the reception of their work. A more helpful response to his remarks might have been a historical overview recognizing the evolution of Latina literature and the unique qualities of Cisneros's work (which Stavans feels is better left to seventh graders) that have made it so important across all borders. Even more important, perhaps, would be an explanation of where, how, and why these works and the realities they depict intersect. As is evidenced in our interviews, this kind of transcanonical analysis is something these writers have revealed as important to them and it is something that can now be of use to us in our analysis of their work. "It is also important for people to enter the reality of a little Mexican-American girl in *The House on Mango Street* or to enter the reality of a Native Americans in *Love Medicine*, just as it's important for them to understand a crazed sea captain on a whaling ship or an indecisive Danish prince," says Alvarez.

This divisive and unproductive territorial ethnicity has been invoked by critics and readers to criticize the work of contemporary Latino writers, men and women. It also explains why many of the writers chose to delete their comments on literary criticism from the interviews published here. Many expressed bewilderment at being considered traitors to their cultures by some readers. This is especially true for the Caribbean writers Julia Alvarez, Cristina García, Judith Ortiz Cofer, Esmeralda Santiago, and Nicholasa Mohr. They have been criticized for having abandoned their homeland, their language, their culture. Santiago had to defend the title of her autobiography, *When I Was Puerto Rican*, several times because her community felt the preterit tense meant that she no longer considered herself part of the culture. Cofer has been accused of not being Puerto Rican, just as García has been accused of not being Cuban enough because she writes in English. Alvarez explains that when she returns to the island she is no longer seen as a "real" Dominican and that now she accepts that she is a "mixture." Mohr, who has seen it all before, responded more than twenty years ago to this kind of cultural balkanization with her important essay, "A Separation Beyond Language." In it she wrote that the separation between the Puerto Rican community on the mainland and that on the island is, without a doubt, "beyond language." It is painful for the writers to talk about, yet they are forthcoming in their analysis and characterization of the exclusionary ethnicity that has left them, in many respects, without a homeland. At the same time the writers are also accused of betraying their community for different reasons. Alvarez and Cisneros have had to fight to remain childless in the face of the cultural demands of Latino society where, as Alvarez points out in her essay "Imagining Motherhood." "being a woman and a mother are practically synonymous." But, as she says in the interview, "there are also other ways to mother and to nurture that do not necessarily have to do with having a child biologically." Perhaps she means creating fiction, perhaps giving back to the community. In *A Portrait of a Queer Motherhood*, Moraga redefines motherhood as a queer mother with a small boy. Being single is seen as another betrayal. Cisneros says she did not realize how hard she had been fighting for unmarried status until the critic Norma Alarcón pointed it out to her. Yet another accusation directed at these Latina writers is that they have abandoned their community in favor of the privileged status of professor. Many try to come to terms with this by being involved in their communities. But, as both Moraga and Cisneros say, the dual role of writer and activist can be exhausting. Cisneros now believes that her writing is the most important gift that she can give back to the community. And she takes this role as seriously as if she were fighting in the streets.

Many of the writers respond to questions about their identity or their homeland in contradictory ways. They worry about being accused of some sort of ethnic impurity by their reading public. Although they are comfortable with themselves and spend little time analyzing their identities, their readers demand of them a certain ethnic conformity. This conflict, between a private identity and a public one, betrays a peculiar isolation among these writers. García simply states that she does not have a geographic identity "that way." Her homeland is on the page: "I'm not sure I know myself except on the page." Ferré's "true habitat" is the "water of words." Cisneros calls herself a translator, an amphibian between two worlds. The most unfortunate consequence of this concern about ethnic orthodoxy is that, as the writers themselves point out, they—not their works of art—have become the objects of examination. All of these writers have made sacrifices in order to develop their literary voices; readers should not dismiss their struggle. However, the focus of criticism should be their work, not their identity or their struggle to achieve it. Perhaps it is time for critics to abandon the hyphenated-identity. If we really listen to what these writers are saying, and to their silences, we will find that they are offering new insights into how to contextualize their work, how to make a place for them in the canon, how to move forward with Latina/Chicana literature.

Our hope is that this book will serve as a segue to a new dialogue in the twenty-first century with regard to Latina/Chicana literature, to the question of where and how this literature will fit in the American literary tradition, and to the many other issues found in these conversations. In the end, whether Latina/Chicana literature finds a permanent place in the canon or not, these voices have held our attention and have contributed to a new literary sensibility. As Alvarez says, speaking on the fate of Latina literature, "Over time a culture uses what it can use and the rest falls away and creates literary fertilizer for the next crop coming up." Undoubtedly this literature will be present in the next generation of writers.

Bridget Kevane

(1)

Citizen of the World

An Interview with Julia Alvarez

Julia Alvarez was born in New York in 1950. She received a B. A. in English at Middlebury College, where she graduated summa cum laude, and earned her M. A. in creative writing at Syracuse University. She spent the first ten years of her life in the Dominican Republic, until her family was forced to move to the United States as political exiles. She now returns often to her homeland. She is currently professor of creative writing and English literature at Middlebury College.

When I met Alvarez at Middlebury College in February 1998, she greeted me with a warm smile and took me to her home. As we drove to her house, we discussed her recent projects, the state of Latino literature, American and Latin American literature, traveling, and a love of good coffee. Sitting in a study room, I noticed bookshelves, plants on her desk, and a window that overlooked the scenic snowcapped mountains of Vermont. As we spoke Alvarez showed me the embroidery and calligraphy of her first collection of poems, The Housekeeping Book. *Her fellow artist friends, members of the Vermont Women's Art Collaborative, had handmade this piece. Alvarez talked about how, as a young writer, she traveled throughout the United States to teach as a poet in the schools and as a visiting professor, often learning from her students' stories.*

After Alvarez published How the García Girls Lost Their Accents *(1991), she came into prominence as a fiction writer. This novel portrays the coming of age of four sisters who leave their home with their family in the Dominican Republic to seek political asylum in the United States. In 1994 Alvarez received a National Book Critic's Award nomination for her novel* In the Time of the Butterflies. *This work captures the heroic struggle of the Mirabal sisters who founded the underground movement against Trujillo's dictatorship. By combining history and fiction, Alvarez demonstrates that some stories are better told through a poetic sensibility than factual documentation. In the novel* ¡YO! *(1997) Alvarez returns to the characters of her first novel, all of whom respond to the protagonist, Yolanda, who is also considered Alvarez's alter ego. With irony and poignancy she chronicles the life of a writer who has achieved success at the expense of criticism from her circle of family and friends.*

All that said, Alvarez is a poet at heart. She has not only written two collections of poems, Homecoming *(1985) and* The Other Side/El Otro Lado *(1995), but she also admires poets of all periods and places. In fact, she pays homage in great depth to Walt Whitman in this interview. In* Something to Declare *(1998), Alvarez gathers a collection of essays on personal experiences and the craft of writing. Before she began to write essays, fiction, or poetry, though, stories occupied an important place in her life as a writer.*

J.H.

JH: What motivated you to become a writer? Is there any connection to your childhood in the Dominican Republican?

I don't think I would have become a writer if I had not come to the United States at the age of ten. I did not have a literary childhood. Seeing people read was a rare thing. I only saw it in school, and I hated books because I did not find much in them that was of interest to me. I was being sent to an American school where we had the Dick and Jane readers in English. This was not my language, and these were not my people. So I was not that interested in those readers. At the same time, though, I think I was in a very storytelling culture. Dominicans are great storytellers! My mother and all the women in my family were great storytellers, so I grew up in a folk culture where stories were very important. But in terms of writing or being one of these bookish people or always having to keep a journal, forget it! When I came into the English language, I discovered books.

JH: Your departure from the Dominican Republic was rather abrupt. How did you feel leaving the homeland?

When my family and I came to the United States, we were really political exiles, as opposed to a large Dominican immigrant population who came around the seventies more for economic reasons. My parents were planning our departure, but it was abrupt and we were not prepared as children. I think it was one of the most traumatic experiences of my life. Suddenly everything changed overnight—the way the air smelled, the way the light felt, the way the people responded, the language in which people responded, the food that was given to us in school, the structure of the family, which was no longer extended and varied but suddenly a nuclear family, which put a lot of pressure on all of us. Before, in the Dominican Republic, among a dozen tías, we had many mothers. Suddenly there was such pressure on Mamí and on each other. That was really hard.

JH: Was the transition to school easier considering the fact that you did attend an American school in the Dominican Republic?

Perhaps . . . But don't forget that U.S.A. street English did not sound the same as classroom, blackboard, verb drill English! When we arrived in New York, I remember having to concentrate to hear the words and not lose the sense at the same time. So I had this sense of anxiety all the time that I would not understand what was being said. I spoke with an accent, which made it hard for people to understand me. I learned to pay attention. So I became very interested in words, the little weights and measures of each word. Why does one say "kind" instead of "generous"? These are the subtleties that you learn as a child when you are learning your mother tongue, almost intuitively, but I was learning a second language as a young girl intentionally. I think this experience was a great influence in my becoming a writer, because I think you have to do that with your own language when you become a writer. That's part of the training and the craft, but I was doing it as a ten-year-old in order to survive in this new country.

JH: I know that you have many sisters. Did you find comfort in their company?

We did not move into a Latino community where there were other people like us, so I really depended on my nuclear family, especially my sisters. Our surroundings were in English, alien to us. All we had was each other. Once Trujillo was killed, we found we had become hybrids, Dominican-Americans! We were no longer "real" Dominicans because we had changed. But we were not mainstream Americans either. We were ni pez, ni carne, neither fish nor fowl. We had experienced situations that our Dominican cousins back on the island had not. Our eyes had seen new things that they had not seen and the same occurred with our U.S.A. friends. We were between worlds. We belonged nowhere. So I sought out books, the homeland of the imagination.

JH: Who were some of your role models in literature? Who were you drawn to?

Well, in high school we were taught the canon that I admired, but I did not connect with these authors. My first chosen mentor was Walt Whitman. He was so, well, so "Latino." In fact, a few years back, I read Borges's Spanish translation of Whitman's *Leaves of Grass*. I thought, my God! I think Whitman wrote *Leaves of Grass* originally in Spanish! The style, the expansiveness, the gestures, the rhetorical way of using this Anglo-Sajón language so that it just rolls off the tongue, the long lines, lush and tropical. No wonder Whitman translates so well into Spanish. Borges does such a wonderful job that I thought, gosh, Whitman is a Latino-American writer. His attitude was also so inclusive. That might have been some of the attraction—a sense of an expansive America that includes so many different kinds of people. If I contradict myself, very well, I contradict myself. I am large. I contain multitudes. That sense of being American, as being diverse: I don't belong in the parlor speaking pretty English. I belong listening to the organ player in the Southern church. I belong wandering the prairies. I belong with the longshoremen in New England. I belong among the Indian prince traveling. It's this sense of inclusiveness that appealed to me because I was part of that America too. I liked his defiance of being trapped within a limited definition of what it was to be American. I think all of that—his gutsiness, his being mar-

ginal, his not wanting to be trapped in a limited self-definition, his wanting to take it all—drew me to him as a writer.

JH: It sounds like a very transient identity, mobile and fluid, moving
through landscapes.

Exactly. His rootlessness was part of his being rooted in this country.
That kind of mobility appealed to me a great deal. I was also very taken
with Emily Dickinson: her intensity, her refusal to be trapped in the
typical paradigm of a young woman of her class. Her exact focus on any
little thing. She would take a feeling of solitude and mourning and zoom
in on exactly how that feels in language. Whitman, Dickinson: I loved
both of their intensities in different ways!

JH: How do you recall this period of the 1960s?

The civil rights movement was just getting started. All those movements—
women's, multicultural—were in the future. That cracking open of American culture,with people who had long been left out saying, "I, too, sing
America," it had not yet happened. Not until college and graduate school
did I feel the social world around me include people like me.

JH: Why did you begin to write poetry before prose fiction?

I think the love of the language, the love of each word. Also, I think the
brevity of form. There are so many words in a novel. I felt that the wild
horses of English would run away with me. I could manage them only
in a small arena. In a poem the heart of the language was there that I had
not gotten as a child in English.

JH: You have to be very precise with language to write poetry, which I
think is more difficult than writing fiction.

A poem is very intimate, heart-to-heart, whereas I think a story weaves
a world that you enter. You can feel close to a character or a situation,
but it's not that intense one-to-one of a lyric poem in which every word
counts. There is nothing else, no narrative world, just the language in a
poem, a voice speaking to you.

JH: You have stated in one of your essays that Maxine Hong Kingston was very important in your formation as a novelist and consciousness as a woman writer.

Reading Maxine Hong Kingston's *Woman Warrior*, I realized that here was a Chinese-American woman with a different background but engaged in the same struggle of trying to put together two different worlds, two different languages, two different ways of seeing things. As I read her memoir, I kept saying, "Yes, yes!" It is beautifully written, a real classic. The book also confronted the demon that I had to confront as well. Maxine's first sentence is "'You must not tell anyone, my mother said,' what I am about to tell you.'" Hey, I thought, my Mamí told me that too! Not just my Mamí, but the whole culture she represented—Catholic, female, Old World, being told to keep my mouth shut, being told to keep things entre familia, never to betray ourselves, and all of those things. Maxine showed me the way out of the tight circle of taboos that I had been raised to observe as a Latina woman.

JH: What did you read later on?

I began to read African-American literature—Toni Morrison, Alice Walker, Zora Neale Hurston. Native American writers, Latino writers. I began to search for the literature I had not been taught in school. I found Rudy Anaya's *Bless Me, Ultima,* Ernesto Galarza's *Barrio Boy*, Eduardo Rivera's *Family Installments*. When I began teaching survey courses, I introduced my students to these books, Latino books. At first I did not find many Latina writers except for Nicholasa Mohr's work, *Nilda*, and Lorna Dee Cervantes's *Emplumada*. Then I found Cherríe Moraga and the Kitchen Table group that came out with *Cuentos: Stories by Latinas*. With that collection I discovered that there were other women, like me, writing from a tradition that incorporated our Latina selves as well as our U.S.A. American selves. At Syracuse University, where I went to graduate school, the women in the program started an alternative workshop and we would meet once a week. All the women discussed the literature that we were writing from a different point of view. That gave me experience outside the academic structure in addressing alternative ways of thinking, writing, and reading. Many of these women gave me recommendations to read this or that. So I became acquainted with a different kind of literature than the traditional canon I had known before. I'm glad I had both of these educations.

JH: Could you elaborate on both of those kinds of education, formal and personal?

Both kinds of knowledge are significant. It's important to understand formal verse, for instance, if you want to write free verse. You have to understand a metrical line when you write free verse. But if you don't know what a metrical line is, how can you "explode" it? What is free verse? What is the sonnet structure, and how do you work inside that structure to claim it for yourself? How do you move within? What kind of new structure do you create? I'm glad I had formal training. I read "the canon" because these paradigms formed the culture that I'm working to reform and expand. For example, I have to know *The Tempest* to fully understand *Caliban*. Before dying in a concentration camp, Robert Desnos, the French poet, said that the task was not only to be oneself but to become each one. I love it!

JH: How did you begin to develop your poetic voice?

I first heard my voice with the *Housekeeping* poems. The stuff I was writing before that sounded stilted, and I had not learned to trust my voice. In that alternative workshop people would tell me to close my eyes and listen to the voice inside me, what does it sound like? I was expecting to hear, "Sing in me, muse, and through me tell the story." But when I closed my eyes what I heard were things like, Don't put so much vinegar in the lettuce, you are going to ruin the salad. You call that a blind stitch? I can't see it. This is the way you make a cake. I heard women talking to me about taking care of a house. That was what I heard growing up, voices of women doing things together in a household.

JH: Well, family is certainly important in your fiction, especially your first novel, *How the García Girls Lost Their Accents*. Do you consider it semiautobiographical?

[Laughs] Oh, don't call it semiautobiographical! You'll get me in trouble with my family. I think first novels are often a kind of bildungsroman.

Young writers are often trying to work out their stories, the world according to how they were raised, the journey that they underwent, almost as if to clear the slate for other things that are coming. So I think definitely my story is part of that first novel. But not only my story, the stories of my people, Latinos who were also Americans, a hybrid. I was especially interested in Latinas who were also dealing with gender issues, issues about being "nice girls" from Latino families who had to deal with the rough and tough new world to which they had come. This story, the story of women like us, was one I had never read before. That's why I felt it was necessary for me to put it down on paper.

JH: And you continue this story with some of the same characters in *¡YO!* creating a dialogue between your works. How did *¡YO!* evolve?

¡YO! is very much a "portrait of the artist." Again, this type of novel follows a very canonical structure: the artist as the aristocrat of spirit is always awarded the point of view. Western literature gives the top position to the artist, especially with romanticism, Wordsworth, and later Joyce and Proust. Well, I've never been interested in hierarchies. That's the reason that I can't stand the placing of "the top Latina writers." I don't like that. It makes me uncomfortable.

In *¡YO!* I took the point of view away from the traditional aristocrat, the artist. I gave it to the "little people" who surround the artist, who tell you they are not creative, not storytellers. But these people, who do not consider themselves artistic, tell stories. Even the people I grew up with in the Dominican Republic, whom I told you were nonliterary, those people told wonderful stories, because all of us need stories to survive. This is how we make our lives meaningful, trying to tell ourselves in our heads the story of who we are.

JH: In the workshops, how do you teach writing? What advice do you give students?

Writing is a craft. All I can do is expose students to good writers and texts and follow their own process and progress as they find their voices. I give them a variety of those texts to read, hoping they'll find what they need to put the world together with language. Look at a de Maupassant story or a Sandra Cisneros story. Look at the different tools the authors use, like point of view. Then you have options. When you write your story, you will have choices and models. But being a writer also involves revision: you have to shape what is meaningful to you into something that is meaningful to the reader too. You have to have models. Many times, young writers just want to write. When I ask them about point of view or character or what they are trying to do with dialogue, they can't really say. They are unaware of the options available to them. They have not read enough. If I want to throw a dinner party in a novel, I might read a scene from Tolstoy's *War and Peace*. But I also try to encourage young writers to find out what they need to write about. What are the stories that they have to tell?

JH: Can you tell which students will be prose writers or poets?

I can tell you if a student has promise because he or she is interested in language. I can't say that this person will be a great novelist, or poet, or journalist, but I can say that there is something there. I can't predict. Look at all of us. Sandra [Cisneros] began as a poet. I began as a poet. So many of us. Judith Ortiz Cofer. Learning and controlling the language is going to work no matter what you do with it. I tell them that good writing is good writing. If you write a good memo, that is good writing too. But it is not art. Art begins with that, but it goes further. I can't tell which ones will go further.

JH: Your novel *In the Time of the Butterflies* pays homage to heroic people, like an ode that reminds me of Keats and Neruda. What made you write this story as a novel instead of poems?

Since writing a novel is a messy job, you don't get a clean notebook and start off. That's what used to scare me about writing novels. I thought that's how "real" writers wrote novels. Well, that's not how I write them. I discard chapters out the window; a framework I thought was going to be the structure of the novel goes out too. But you remind me that I did begin that novel by writing poems in the voices of each of the characters. Each sister had a poem before each chapter. I envisioned that those poems would form part of the novel, and then the poems fell away. I still have them in folders. I guess I needed them in order to hear essentially, rhythmically, each voice. The sound of each voice came to me via poetry.

JH: What motivated you to write this novel about a specific event in Dominican history?

When I met the surviving Mirabal sister, Dedé, in the Dominican Republic, I realized that I was actually going to write a novel. Before that the Mirabal sisters were legends. But when I met Dedé, I saw the clothes that her sisters were wearing the day they were killed. I held María Teresa's braid that Dedé had cut off before the burial; I saw their bedrooms, sat on their beds. I felt the sisters come to life in all those details that Dedé shared with me. They became real to me because she was real. She was really my entry into the story. Then I also heard stories from other members of their family, from people who had been in the underground with them. I gathered all these pieces together. Their voices became real to me in an intuitive way. Each one would require something different of me. Patria liked me to read her the Bible. María Teresa liked girls' diaries. Anne Frank, of course. The novel had to end with the sisters still being alive. The murder scene would have taken over the whole novel and would have been what my readers remembered. I wanted the readers to remember their lives, not their deaths. Also, I wanted the readers, like Dedé, the survivor, to have to make sense of their stories.

JH: I can see resemblances to novels about resistance to dictatorships in Latin America or literature of the Holocaust. Which books influenced you in this process?

Certainly I was influenced by literature of the Holocaust and the testimonial literature that comes out of Latin America—that whole tradition, the Mothers of the Plaza in Argentina. I did a lot of reading of women in the Resistance in France during World War II. A lot of the reading I did is not a part of North American literature, except for the narratives of slavery. Political testimonial literature does not come from the U.S.A. tradition. It just goes to show that as a writer I am a mixture of traditions.

JH: How did you feel when you received the National Book Critics' Award nomination for *Butterflies*? Do you sense an impact in the direction of American literature?

When I saw the nomination for the National Book Critics' Award, I was shocked, but I tried to put it out of my mind to stay focused on my work. Book biz can be distracting. A writer runs the danger of becoming a creature of publicity. You asked me if I like to go on book tours. It's so easy to get sucked into that star world instead of paying attention to your work. And your work is really bigger than you. The canon is widening to include Julia Alvarez, Sandra Cisneros, Rudolfo Anaya, essentially books that can help because they are deeply meaningful, not just to Latinos, but to all of us as a culture. For me to have read *The Invisible Man* is to have become an African-American. It makes me more of a human being. I enter another reality. That's why the canon should include all of us. It is also important for people to enter the reality of a little Mexican-American girl in *The House on Mango Street* or to enter the reality of Native Americans in *Love Medicine*, just as it's important for them to understand a crazed sea captain on a whaling ship or an indecisive Danish prince. You don't exclude those points of views or those realities. You also don't include books because they present "other" realities but because they are fine books, and they belong there along with the canonical "classics."

JH: What is your present relationship with the Dominican Republic?

Well, Bill [Alvarez's husband] and I have started a project. Coming from there, being one of the lucky ones, having had a good education and having achieved all these things that I had as dreams, that I never thought I could achieve, all of this means that I have a responsibility to give something back. How do I serve now in this part of my life? What Bill and I are starting there is a model farm that will have an artist center for Dominicans. These artist "colonies" exist in this country—a place where a Dominican painter can come and paint for a couple of months. What will be required of the residents is that they do something for the community. They could give a workshop or donate a piece of work that would be part of the foundation so that it can make money to support itself. They could work on the farm, using organic methods that take care of the land. So that's my goal, trying to be a part of both worlds but also trying to do the cross-semination that is already in my work now in terms of the places that I move in.

JH: In your groundbreaking essay, "On Finding a Latino Voice," you discuss the need to form a literary tradition. You pose the question, "Why couldn't we have a made-in-the-U.S.A. Latino and Latina literary boom"? What do you think happened in the 1990s, and where do you see it going?

Well, I think what happened is the same thing that happened with African-American literature. Suddenly there was a "discovery" of Richard Wright, Maya Angelou. Suddenly Alice Walker, Toni Morrison, Gloria Naylor, and Ntzoke Shange. The voices were there, but "suddenly" the publishing establishment noticed. And one by one, each voice adds to the critical mass and there is a "boom." You put certain numbers together, and an energy is born that is bigger than the individual parts. Sandra Cisneros, Ana Castillo, Cherríe Moraga, Lorna Dee Cervantes, and Judith Ortiz Cofer, some of us were in touch here and there with one another. But suddenly there was this sense of energy from conversation and dialogue, a chorus that started building, all of these voices in all their diversity, how much we share and how different we all are. On the market level what happened was that publishers realized that these writers really sell and some of them are terrific writers. In this boom there are definitely books and writers whose works are not as strong. Some books will stay, and the others will sink to the bottom. But, as I often tell my students, maybe some of these stories are not so good, but they have to write those stories to get to their best stories. Over time a culture uses what it can use and the rest falls away and creates literary fertilizer for the next crop coming up.

JH: Do you see a younger generation coming up?

Oh, yeah! Junot Díaz! A Dominican. He is a very talented, wonderful writer. Edwidge Danticat. She is Haitian-American, young, twenty-eight years old. A second wave is now coming up. I think their talent would have thrust them forward, but I think that the market is also ready to receive them because some groundbreaking happened with my generation. Nicholasa Mohr and Lorna Dee Cervantes were the first ones out there, clearing ground. Then Sandra Cisneros, Ana Castillo, Denise Chávez, Cherríe Moraga, Helena María Viramontes, and the rest of us came. Now, new blood! We are taken seriously now as American writers, not as writers of sociological interest only.

JH: In another essay, "Imagining Motherhood," I thought of the pressures involved in being a writer and a mother. How do you feel about these issues?

In my book of essays, *Something to Declare*, I was writing both personal essays and essays about craft. "Imagining Motherhood" was one of the first essays in which I was trying to come to terms with being childless, especially as a Latina. As you know, this is an important "credential" as a Latina. You have to have your children. I had to come to terms with that, not just as a Latina, but as a woman of an earlier generation in which I was told that was something I was supposed to do. What does it mean to be a "childless woman"? Even the role of stepmother, my present role, has such a bad legacy. What does it mean to make a choice not to have a child and still be a whole woman? All the feelings that come to mind and all the pressures and opinions because I made that choice haunt me! I wrote the essay to address those demons that haunt me, to exorcise them. Where does that hunger to be a mother come from? Part of it as a writer is that you want to know everything. You hunger for experience. That desire was driving me too. There are also other ways to mother and to nurture that do not necessarily have to do with having a child biologically.

JH: Do you feel close to your family now?

Oh, yes, both with my sisters here and with my family in the Dominican Republic. Some of my Dominican family have made very different choices about their lifestyles, their values, how they decide to spend their time. I am sure they find it absolutely crazy for my husband and me to buy land up in the mountains, where there is no electricity, no good roads, no phones, no running water. And here we are, trying to grow organic coffee and be part of a comunidad. But family is always family. I think it's a gene that I got as being part of that culture, that familia is important even if people are different from me. We all belong. Everybody is part of la familia—el loco, la jamona. [Laughs] I do keep up when we go down there, always staying at my favorite tía's house in the capital, visiting the cousins that drop in. Now that we have our own place up in the mountains, we have our own base and connections with people there who are not necessarily family. We already feel a part of this other community, very much so.

JH: What feels like home for you?

As Czeslaw Milosz said in a quote I used as the epigraph to *Homecoming*, my book of poems, "Language is the only homeland." The page is where I've learned to put together my different worlds, where I've put down the deepest roots. Maybe because I am an immigrant, I don't feel those deep loyalties to a piece of land or a landscape. But the world of the imagination is the one I feel most at home in. I am a traveler with this portable homeland of the imagination.

JH: Is that how you would like to be remembered, a traveler?

Yes, a traveler. The writer Terence, born a slave, once said, "I am a human being. Nothing human is alien to me." Not only to be oneself, but to be each one. These phrases mean a great deal to me. What I try to do with my writing is to move out into those other selves, other worlds. To become more and more of us. Here, I am writing in English often about Dominican situations and characters, using Spanish as part of my English—those combinations are happening all over the planet, as populations are on the move. I find this empowering: that we are becoming these mixtures, we are becoming each other. By allowing myself to be those mixtures and not having to choose or repress myself or cut myself off from the other, I have become a citizen of the world.

(2)
The Spirit of Humor

An Interview with Denise Chávez

Denise Chávez was born in Las Cruces, New Mexico, in 1948. She developed a love of writing as a form of self-empowerment at the age of eight. This apprenticeship did not lead her directly into fiction writing but rather into the world of drama and theater. She was able to explore acting in terms of characterization, dialogue, and humor, elements that she would use in her prose fiction. If there is one thing that Chávez has a gift for, it is laughter. We were able to speak to her by telephone in June 1996 and in March 1998. She tells us in the interview, "With humor, you can say some very deep things. Life has its sorrows and its tragedies, but humor is something that tempers the bitterness, the hard edges of life. You keep surviving. That's the Mexican spirit!"

By earning scholarships to study acting, Chávez was able to work with professors from Greece, Russia, and Puerto Rico. She recalls these days as exciting moments when she learned to appreciate the intensity, discipline, and gregariousness of her first mentors. But it was not until she heard of and saw the work of Rudolfo Anaya, one of the godfathers of Chicano literature, that Chávez became determined to declare herself as a writer to the universe. In other words, she wanted to become a serious writer. She has earned an M.F.A. in drama from Trinity University and an M. A. in creative writing from the University of New Mexico. As a writer of New Mexico, she considers landscape a special element in her fiction, The Last of the Menu Girls *(1986)* and Face of an Angel *(1994). She is also concerned with issues of family, culture, young adolescents turning to womanhood, and living in the borderlands of two cultures. In her novel* Loving Pedro Infante *(2000), Chávez addresses the impact of Mexican cinema on a generation of women in the United States as well as in Mexico.*

Apart from writing prose fiction, Chávez also writes plays for youngsters and adults. Her plays have been produced throughout the United States and Europe, including the Edinburgh Festival and the Festival Latino de Nueva York through Joseph Papp. "Woman in the State of Grace" is a one-woman show that she occasionally performs on the road. She has presented readings and workshops for students K-12, college students, the elderly, the developmentally disabled, at-risk, underserved audiences, and prisoners. In 1996 Chávez won the Luminaria Award, presented by the New Mexico Community Foundation in Santa Fe to twelve New Mexicans whose philanthropic work and values effect positive change in communities throughout the state. She also earned a 1996 Woman of Distinction award in education from the Soroptimist International of the Americas Club.

Chávez is currently assistant professor of creative writing at New Mexico State University. She has been the artistic director of the Border Book Festival, a major regional book festival based in Las Cruces, since its inception in 1994. She is deeply committed to her community in Las Cruces and hopes to leave a legacy for future generations. The interview begins with her reflection on how she began to write.

J.H.

JH: How did you begin to write? Were you young?

I always kept a diary. I started writing when I was eight years old. I've always had diaries and journals. I have always loved writing. Writing, for me, is a natural extension of thinking. The greatest experience was to go into my diary. Later on, in junior high and high school, I started transcribing other people's writings. I really liked putting my favorite poems into my journal. After that I found myself writing a lot of poetry and stories. I can't say that I studied writing. I naturally had to find my own voice. I attribute my love for writing to the fact that I spent so much time by myself from such an early age. Writing was a way to communicate, explain, understand, and empower myself. That's how I really began to know I was a writer. My secret ambition at age ten was to become a writer.

JH: What were you interested in writing about?

As an adolescent, I was interested in writing about finding love, keeping it, finding happiness, finding my way in the world. I didn't know what I wanted to dedicate my life to. I was interested in family, and creating characters. I wanted to find my roots. I've always been very loyal to my community, my state, and the people I grew up with. In a play I wrote in college, called *The Wait*, I wrote about leaving home, moving on and doing other things. I started acting in high school. That's when I realized theater was also a communication tool.

JH: How did you like acting?

I started acting as a sophomore in high school. I found that I had a knack for it. It was an amazing recognition for me that I may have some talent. I found a direction when I began acting. I knew that I could write, but I had never seen the flowering of my writing in any form. Acting was instantaneous communication. I started getting roles in high school. I won a scholarship to New Mexico State University when I was a senior in high school for my role as the grandmother in a play called *Grey Bread*. It was the best actress award that gave me a scholarship in theater. The award elevated me to an incredible level of commitment and awareness. I'll never forget the night I received the award. It seemed my life was on a trajectory that was really exciting! Plus, I loved theater. In fact, in college I practically lived in the drama department.

JH: What kinds of roles did you enjoy the most?

Well, I enjoyed a variety. We happened to have a Russian director, Hershel Zohn. He acted in New York in Yiddish theater. He was very interested in the Russian masters, particularly Chekhov. So I played Sonya in *Uncle Vanya*. That was the female lead. And there I was, a mocosa! I must have been seventeen years old. That role catapulted me to a level of tremendous energy! I think one of my personal favorites, as far as roles go, was Varya in *The Cherry Orchard*. We did everything! You name it. We did

Gorky, Shakespeare, many classics. I took courses in modern European drama, modern American drama, Restoration comedy, and the Greeks. I loved the work of Eugene O'Neill. I've read most of his work, including all the obscure plays. I also liked the work of Lillian Hellman. My background in theater was really a preparation for my work as a fiction writer. It was a great training ground for any kind of writer to read such incredible world drama. Chekhov is the master of characterization as far as I am concerned.

JH: Your training as an actress had an impact on your fiction writing as well. Would you agree?

Absolutely. You have to know your characters. You work with detail, gesture, color, intonation, and silence. I am very interested in rhythm. The reading that I like always has music in it. It's not enough to tell a story. I am interested in the voice of the story, the characterization inherent in voice. I am really grateful that I had my background in theater. A lot of the people who moved me then were male writers. Federico García Lorca is perhaps a major influence because he was not only a masterful poet but also a theater person. A play like *Blood Wedding*, in which I once played the bride. It does not get much better than that.

JH: The drama complements the humor and comedy in your works also.

Very much so. Aristophanes's play *The Birds* is a wonderful comedy, a parody. Humor helps so much. With humor you can say so many deep and powerful things. When I moved on to the Dallas Theatre Center as an actress in graduate school, we had a Greek director, Takis Muzenidis, and a Greek dancing coach. I was in the women's chorus of *Lysistrata* directed by these two intensely fierce Greek people. It was so rigorous. The dance coach was a slave driver. We rehearsed for months, dancing, singing. It was an incredible experience! I have also acted Chekhov in Spanish. I worked with a very well known director from Puerto Rico, Mr. Leo Lavandero. I've had wonderful theater experiences. I've taken classes with Megan Terry, José Quintero, and Edward Albee. Edward Albee and I were colleagues at the University of Houston when I taught acting there. I never thought in my wildest dreams that I would share an office with Edward Albee! Theater was an enormous education for me.

JH: You eventually left drama. Why did you make this decision?

I keep myself away from it because it's a very draining lifestyle. It's hard to be in rehearsal every single night. I chose not to do that. I chose to be a fiction writer. There was a very strong split for me. I love the theater madly, but I don't want to live the life of a full-time theater person. Every night at rehearsal. Living in L.A. or New York. I chose instead to work theater into my fiction.

JH: Yes, I've noticed. What brings out the comedian in you, which is also evident in your writing?

Oh, my God! What a question! I grew up with a lot of funny people. My father had a wonderful wit. He was very comical. His timing was impeccable. He was a lawyer, and he was a good speaker. He had a powerful voice. My mother was very bright and also had a great sense of humor. Her delivery was fantastic. When you grow up with people who appreciate laughter, you can't help but learn from them. My family was a great education. I came to appreciate the power of humor. I love to laugh, and I love to be around people who are funny and make me laugh. With humor, you can say some very deep things. Life has its sorrows and its tragedies, but humor is something that tempers the bitterness, the hard edges of life. You keep surviving. That's the Mexican spirit. Ni modo, you keep on going. You can have a wicked sense of humor when you're down and out and in the mud. You can laugh at the absurdity of life and the craziness. I never want to leave humor behind. It's who I am!

BK: What contemporary American writers do you have a connection with?

I love the work of Dagoberto Gilb, who used to live in El Paso. He's a terrific writer. His short stories are profound and show the inner life of working-class people, laborers. I also love the work of Sandra Cisneros. What's so wonderful about Latino writers is that we are moving forward together, compañeros in la lucha de arte y literatura. That's what the writer Jim Sagel said, and it's so. To be a Latino writer is to write the collaborative story. Another favorite writer is Terry Tempest, a feminist Mormon from Salt Lake. Her book, *Refuge*, is a testimony to all the women in her family who have died from breast cancer, including her mother.

Her work is very moving on a very spiritual level and on a very deep heart level. I think she is a wonderful storyteller. I met her years ago and love her as a friend and sister. There are so many good writers, and most of them have this orality I speak of that lifts the words off the page and allows them to sing.

JH: Which Latin American writers have affected you?

Juan Rulfo. Oh my God, *Pedro Páramo* is a masterpiece. I remember the first time I read it. Rulfo had a way of distilling time and space and the human heart. I love the way Tomás Rivera took Rulfo's energy and wrote *Y no se lo tragó la tierra*, his choral piece that would make a great opera. You can see the lines of connection between Rulfo and Rivera and then move on to Alberto Ríos in *Pig Cookies and Other Stories*. *Pig Cookies* is so innovative and fresh. The books I've mentioned will never age. They have an energy that is timeless.

JH: Speaking of short stories, how did you begin writing *The Last of the Menu Girls*, your first published collection?

When I was about twenty-four, things started to coalesce for me. I had to make a declaration to myself that I was going to be a writer. This is what I wanted to do for the rest of my life. I literally went outside and declared myself to the universe. I ritualized my becoming a writer. And I encourage my writers to do the same. When I teach creative writing I ask my students to make a verbal ritualistic commitment to themselves and the spirits, to all life.

JH: How do you look back on this first collection of fiction?

It's like a beautiful child. You look at them and love them deeply. I'm very proud of that work. Rocío is a wonderful character. The book is about Rocío's coming of age. I wrote it in a time of my life when I was setting out as well. The book is about a young woman coming into her own in the Southwest. In a way it epitomized the spirit that I felt and that I wanted to talk about. I have moved from there. You can't help but have a tenderness for those places and those characters that reflect some part of yourself that existed. It certainly was a wonderful experience to work on those stories.

JH: Did anyone encourage you to become a writer at this time?

One day Rudolfo Anaya approached me. I had submitted a short story to the collection *Cuentos Chicanos,* and he liked it. He cornered me and asked, "So, what are you going to do now?" I took it as a challenge. What I imagined he meant was, "Are you going to write or WHAT and WHEN are you going to get started?" At that time the University of New Mexico had started a graduate fellowship in Creative Writing. I was one of the first recipients. One could get a master's degree in one year! I did, but it was a brutal year. I was living in Santa Fe and commuting. I got walking pneumonia. I had a lot of parking tickets and was always late for class. It was only through Rudy's prodding and encouragement and my own stubbornness that I made it. My master's thesis was *The Last of the Menu Girls*, a collection of seven interrelated short stories. This was the first time that I had ever put anything together into some kind of form. When I was eight years old, I wrote my first story about a willow tree. Later, at twenty-four, I wrote the story "Willow Game." My writing life didn't begin overnight. It was a maturation process like the growth of a tree. Writing takes a lot of time and reflection. It's a process that demands so much. The seeds of darkness will eventually flower if you are patient and blessed.

BK: Why was it so important to proclaim that commitment to yourself like that?

It's important to ritualize life. For example, we do that in the marriage ceremony, during an anniversary or a birthday, and most especially at death. I see life in terms of progression, movement and cycles. The yearning to be an artist was so deeply ingrained in my being, it became my way to communicate. I became my own priestess in effect. That was the only way that I knew I could make it. I had to lay myself out to the universe. To "postulate provision." I had no idea how I was going to make a living, but I knew I had to become a writer. I thought initially that I might teach drama in high school or college. I believe that if you allow yourself to do what you love, the universe will provide for you. My ritual was really a prayer. Life is a great mystery with its attendant magic. I trusted that my sincerity and commitment would uplift me. You have to absolutely trust you are doing the right thing when you do your ritual to the universe.

JH: Could you talk about the writing process and its effects on you?

The duende comes to us and speaks to us. All of us wait for this moment of clarity and understanding. And of decision. The job of the writer is to define those moments of understanding through the process of words. Writers live for these moments of clarity. As Megan Terry, the playwright, said, and which I believe is so true, "We are all of us writing our way toward mental health." But writing is more than mental or physical health, it's the sanctity of grace to me. I use the word "grace" a lot. It's a grace to be able to understand the sorrows and joys that affect and afflict us. And a grace to be called upon to voice the many inarticulate cries that not only belong to you but to others as well.

BK: Cisneros says she writes to get rid of the obsessions and ghosts that haunt her. What is it for you?

I wrote somewhere in a journal, "I write to set the spirits in motion to be freed." Unless things are moving, there is stagnation.

BK: In *Face of an Angel*, even though people are inside, you can sense this connection with the outside world, the exterior landscape.

I'm glad you feel that, because I wanted to connect with the exterior landscape. I live in a very hot place, on La Frontera, forty-two miles from the Mexican border. I wanted my readers to feel the heat, to smell the enchiladas in El Farol Restaurant, and to feel the restless energy that surrounds you in such a place. It's quite troublesome when the weather does not settle down the way you think it should and the outside is not what you want it to be. There is a certain friction there that is interesting to me. I've never really articulated this, but my exterior landscape is who I am inside. I've lived in a hard place and I wouldn't have it any other way.

BK: Is the Dosamantes family an autobiographical representation?

The Dosamantes family lives in their own reality, in their own world. It is my family in the sense that I love them and have lived with them in the process of writing their stories, but no, they are not my family. My family's story is another story. People come up to me and say that such and such a character reminds them of their aunt or uncle. It's wonderful when a reader is so involved in their own family that your special family becomes their family. I'd like to write the biographies of my parents. I hope to someday. My father was a lawyer and my mother was a teacher. I thank them both for their love and support. They both loved literature. And they were both intelligent, fierce, and unique people. *Face of an Angel* is a tribute to their spirits. But the characters in the book breathe their own air and have their own names.

BK: One of the important themes is also the official history versus the real history of the Dosamantes. Could you elaborate on that?

There are a lot of taboos in culture. If there are incestuous relationships, or sexual improprieties, these things are never brought up. There is also an untold history of a person's life. There's the woman who had a child before she was married, the uncle who was mentally ill, the imbecile child, the retarded sister. Most people don't want to talk about these things on a larger, societal level. I have been one to never shy away from taboos or what people call stereotypes. I believe we can use both to get to the truth. The real story is the story of the heart, nothing more. And in the heart story, there are no lies.

BK: Why do you think readers are so intent on knowing if it's autobiographical?

Readers are curious. We want the work we read to be the life we imagine. But sometimes we forget that the work overcomes the small limitations of an individual life and becomes the greater life, the universal life. That's what any writer wants, to take the leap to tell the universal story. As readers and as people who love chisme and a good story, we are interested in personal details. We are voyeurs of the telenovela, of our neighborhood soaps. It's human to want to know the nitty-gritty. We are all amateur psychoanalysts. We think we know better than the person next to us. We like secrets, we like to figure out the darkness and many reasons. I've had people get disappointed when they're not in something I write. I'm sorry about that.

BK: Two sentences that really struck me are, "The stories begin with the men and always end with the women. That's the way it is in our family." Could you elaborate on your female perspective and female God?

I grew up with God being male. He was the harsh father God that had the fire coming out of his eyes. He stood on a cloud with gold rays emanating from his body. I never really understood that God could be female, with a female spirit or with female body parts. I grew up with a confused idea of what spirituality was. I began to amend the conception of God as I grew older. I began to understand that women could have freedom, that they could be strong and spiritual. They did not have to buy into the concept of a powerful macho father God. Material attainment and power are no longer God to me, or the pursuit of money. The book began to look at how the chains of female oppression could be undone. The novel empowers women to break the legacy of self-persecution. Fortunately, I grew up with a mother who was able to allow me to express myself. She gave me the gift of freedom to do and be what I wanted. Since she had served men all her life, I didn't need to repeat her painful lessons. My mother's gift to me was the gift of her woman's strength. The scene at the end of *Face of an Angel* is the breaking of the ancestral bread, the communion of women. I love the moment of quiet tenderness in that scene and the peace it brings.

JH: What made you decide that *Face of an Angel* would be a novel and not another short story?

Everything has its form. The story was so big that it required a lot of space. It had a cast of thousands. There were so many characters that bit the dust too! The story needed space and time and demanded much movement. I love the characters. Characters are my propelling impetus in writing. I love the women in *Face of an Angel*. I think they are terrific people. To this day, I'm learning from them. I still feel a great affection for them. I don't have a desire to write a sequel, although I think I could. But why? That world is complete for me. And sacred. I just finished working on a novel called *Loving Pedro Infante*.

JH: That is so interesting for me, because I grew up watching his movies and Mexican cinema of that period.

I did too. For Mexicanos and Mexicanas, Pedro Infante was the embodiment of male beauty. His death was a great blow to the world. My book details a long-standing love affair between two people who should not love each other, but do. Their love is so explosive and dangerous and magical that they can only get together every once in a while. When they do get together, everything falls apart for them. The book is about loving, what love really means. Pedro Infante figures in the book, and there is a Pedro Infante fan club as well. Pedro Infante could not only sing, he could act and ride a horse, and he loved more women than you can count. Pedro's life was tragic in many ways, very unstable and confused in many ways, but very interesting as well. *Pedro Infante* is more of a chamber piece, whereas *Face of an Angel* is an opera.

JH: Why did you decide to portray the past of the 1940s and 1950s?

History is very important for me. I grew up with Pedro Infante's movies. The romantic dreams and types of relationships I saw in those movies were part and parcel of who I was, what I wanted in life, or so I thought. Those films have influenced generations of men and women in Mexico and the United States, as well as all around the world. I am only now beginning to understand the dreams of my ancestors and the women and men of my world. The questions I ask myself are, Are my dreams my mother's and father's dreams? Or my grandparent's dreams? What are the contemporary dreams? What does it mean to love someone? In my novel I explore the nature of real love, as opposed to the illusion of love, a celluloid phantasmal love.

JH: Could you see teaching as a way of enhancing your writing? Do you have a relationship with younger writers?

I am a teacher and a student at all times. My students have taught me so much—more than I believe I've taught them. I do believe in mentorship. I have had so many fine teachers, and I pay them homage by continuing my own work.

JH: What feels like home to you? What is your community?

My house and neighborhood are home. The street that I grew up on is home. I love my community. I am very active in my world. I am the director of the Border Book Festival in Las Cruces. Next year will be our fifth year. We bring in writers from all over the United States and Mexico. Expanding the horizons of literature and story and getting people involved is my work as well. I am a community artist, a grassroots person. I hope to leave a legacy of creativity. It's important for me to leave something for those who follow, for posterity. Maybe the Border Book Festival will be part of that. I'd like to leave a house or two for writers to live and work in. I hope that after I'm gone there will be an energy that continues to celebrate this place that I love so much.

(3)

A Home in the Heart

An Interview with Sandra Cisneros

Born in Chicago in 1954 to a Mexican father and a Mexican-American mother, Sandra Cisneros remembers how her parents contributed to the craft of her writing through language. Cisneros says in our interview, "[My mother] has a working-class Chicago voice that is the antithesis of my father's voice. My father is very much the lyrical voice in my writing, the child's voice in my writing. But that child's voice to me is so much part of our Mexican Spanish." Undoubtedly the mixture of colloquial English and lyrical Spanish voices is what characterizes the language and rhythm of Cisneros's poetry and prose. In essence she opened doors for other Latina writers as a precedent setter in both her linguistic experimentation and her celebration of women, that is her devotion to writing about the life experiences of women from their perspectives.

Cisneros began her widely acclaimed first work of fiction, The House on Mango Street *(1984), when she was a graduate student in the M.F.A. program at the Iowa Writers' Workshop in the mid-1970s. In our interview she tells us of the journey she took to finish this work of poetic prose about a young Latina coming of age in Chicago. In* My Wicked Wicked Ways *(1987), Cisneros enters a second phase as she addresses the theme of the single Latina in search of freedom. But it is with* Woman Hollering Creek *(1991) that she explores a wide spectrum of the Mexican community on both sides of the U.S.-Mexican border.* Loose Woman *(1994) presents another turning point as*

Cisneros jumps into the fire of womanhood, because as she says, she is "nobody's mother and nobody's wife."

In public Cisneros does not merely recite her poetry and stories but instead captures her audience's attention through her dramatic readings and modulations. Her frankness, drama, and humor are pivotal elements that enhance her oral performance. In fact, Cisneros has come to appreciate the power of the spoken word through the storytelling that she has been exposed to in her travels in Mexico. She discusses the impact of these stories in the writing of her novel Caramelo, *a tribute to her father and the immigrant experience.*

Cisneros did not always earn her living as a writer, though. Positions as an alternative high school teacher, as a counselor, and as a writer-in-residence at universities also formed part of her apprenticeship. She mentions that she is always aware of people's voices, whether they issue forth in the form of gang slang, or the casual conversation of girlfriends at the laundromat, or the curious Britishisms of Jane Austen's characters. The range of voices has come together for Cisneros in San Antonio, where she is a volunteer teacher at the Guadalupe Cultural Arts Center. As a recipient of the MacArthur award, she has been able to organize Latino recipients, or MacArturos (as Cisneros calls them), into a coalition that shares its expertise with the community via workshops, readings, and performances. She examines the impact of organizing groups "across disciplines, across generations, across sexualities" in "The Genius of Creative Flexibility," published in the Los Angeles Times *in February 1998. Cisneros currently resides in her controversially purple house in a historic district of San Antonio. We were able to speak with Cisneros by telephone twice, in April 1996 and January 1998. We begin with a return to the past as Cisneros remembers her childhood.*

J.H.

JH: Knowing that your father was Mexican and your mother is Mexican-American, could you begin by talking about how this experience affected you as a child?

You could say I remember moving a lot between Chicago and Mexico City in the fifties and sixties. I visited Mexico when I was very young. We were a commuter family, but not any more so than my relatives or neighbors. I remember a time in my life when I wanted to make connections with people. But to tell you the truth, sometimes when people would poke me out of my solitude, I would wish they were not there. I liked spending time by myself more than anything until I was an adolescent. I did drawings and made things. I was always creating, imagining and inventing. I was an artist. I spent a lot of time daydreaming, a kind of fantasy world. It was certainly lots of flights of the imagination that transformed my environment.

JH: What did you enjoy reading as a youngster?

I was a fan of *Alice in Wonderland*. I basically liked books that dealt with the lives of young girls in another age, especially the Victorian or turn-of-the-century period. That fascinated me. I never liked to read about the near past or my mother's childhood because it was too familiar. That was boring for me. You had to go back to the beginning of the century or the last quarter century or even beyond, as in *The Little House on the Prairie* series where they spoke in an odd way. For example, *Alice in Wonderland* has a curious British intonation. The language and dress were curious to me. Those were the kinds of books I liked, the ones that were set in what I then called "the olden times." It had to be distant. I was not really a reader of poetry as a child. The poems I read came surreptitiously through writers like Lewis Carroll. Basically I was a reader of prose, but poetry came to me through some very bad examples in my school textbooks, sing-songy things. Maybe it was fortunate that Lewis Carroll saved me, because I started writing poems with fixed meter. But I did the fixed meter by ear. I did not scan it out. I wrote by ear as if it were a song. But I was basically then a visual artist.

JH: When did you become interested in poetry?

I met the Spanish poets who influenced a generation of North American poets via my high school Spanish teacher. They influenced the direction of my first writings. In undergraduate school I was influenced by Pablo Neruda, Octavio Paz, Federico García Lorca, Juan Ramón Jiménez—Latin American and Spanish lyrical poets. I think I have always been moved by two things in poetry, its power to take one very quickly to an emotional level in few words and its lyrical quality.

JH: How is poetry different from fiction for you?

Poetry is much more rooted in my real life. The autobiographical elements stay pretty much intact. One person can influence one poem; it's as if you are overhearing a phone conversation with me. In fiction I am very conscious of speaking of an issue to the public. I am concerned with a story that I have told verbally to friends or that has caught my attention. I realize that a story has the power to quiet a listener, and I develop that. Sometimes it's an anecdote, but it has to have the power to make people listen. A story arrives in verbal form to me, whereas a poem is much more of an emotion in which I have to search for the language.

JH: What kind of poetic voice were you aiming for in *My Wicked Wicked Ways*? How is *Loose Woman* different?

My Wicked Wicked Ways is an earlier work. I would say it was more like classical music. It is different from *Loose Woman,* which is more like jazz. I see the first work as being very fixed and formal and influenced by my training at the Iowa Writers' Workshop. There are tighter and tauter lines in *My Wicked Wicked Ways*. It is more like ballet. There is a terse quality to the lines. *Loose Woman* has a more colloquial flavor to me, it's even vulgar at times. The lines are loose. Everything is loose. The subjects are loose. I say things that one would not consider proper to say in poetry. It's like I got the workshop, the Church, and everybody else off my back. It's a much looser, freer, jazzier voice in these newer poems, *Loose Woman*.

JH: Have you met Julia Alvarez or Cristina García, who praise you for *Loose Woman* on the back cover?

I met Cristina García on paper. She wrote a note to me. Julia, of course, I know personally now. I knew her first as a poet and was so moved by her first book of poetry, *Homecoming*. I wrote her a fan letter. She was teaching in Illinois, and I was working here in San Antonio. I was enamored of a Latina writing about issues that were close to me with the craftsmanship that I admired, that I aspired to, and I wrote to tell her that. We corresponded later once we both started publishing our works. We came into contact via our mutual agent, I believe, at a reading. By then I knew her works of fiction. We have been corresponding. It seems like I've known her for a long time. Now I feel very close to her. She has been to my home. We don't see each other that often, but because we share an agent, we always send notes or messages. Sometimes we send postcards to each other or regalitos to help us along with our writing. We try not to write or call each other when we are working because we know how upsetting it is to be disturbed and to stop writing.

BK: What were you experiencing in writing *The House on Mango Street*?

So much is unconscious when I was writing. I was very, very young. I was forming both my spirituality and my politics at the time that Esperanza was. If you had asked me these questions at the time I was writing it, I would not have been able to articulate it as spiritual and political. I just knew that there were many things that I felt very powerless to change, things that I was moved by, things I was learning as I was working in the community. As I learned those lessons, they emerged in my text. I was just writing from my heart.

JH: How do you reflect on *The House on Mango Street*, your first piece of prose fiction?

I will probably write other things in that child's voice because that is the voice that comes very easily to me. I would like to continue with children's books, adults' books, other projects. At the time I wrote *Mango Street*, Esperanza was facing issues that were very pressing to a woman in her twenties living in the barrio with young women very unlike herself. In one respect I was raised in the barrio, but I was kind of a princess too. I was protected the way a lot of people can grow up in very harsh neighborhoods, very sheltered. Because you are in the middle of all that violence, your parents make you lead a very sheltered life. You can be poor and sheltered. Because you grew up around gangs, that does not mean that you are a gang member. I was witnessing them but not partaking in them. However, the students I later taught in my twenties were the ones who had been in gangs and done drugs. They lived real lives compared to my good-girl sheltered Catholic life. In my twenties I asked myself, how come this did not happen to me? Or, how can I change these girls' lives? They are my students. They have so many more troubles than I have. I was really a wealthy girl compared to them. In *Mango Street* I felt my own outrage and my responsibility; those are what my issues were at that time. Each book that I write is concerned with whatever I am obsessed with at that time. The book that parallels it is *My Wicked Wicked Ways*. It deals more explicitly with the autobiographical issues of my life. *Mango Street* is an invented autobiography with elements from different parts of my life and extended into my students' lives and the voice of my life in the twenties. As a beginning novelist, I was very interested in condensed forms like Borges's *Dreamtigers*; yet I could not handle many characters in a small form.

JH: Were you aware that your feminist consciousness was being developed at this time?

I think my feminist consciousness was born the moment Norma Alarcón [critic of Chicana literature] stepped into my apartment. I met her when I was invited to read at Bloomington, Indiana, and stayed at her house. She was on the committee that had asked me to come. In those times, people invited you to stay at their house. There was no money for hotels or anything. Then, when she came to Chicago, she stayed with me at my apartment. I remember the day she arrived. She looked around and did not see any children's toys or a man's things and asked, "You live here by yourself?" I said, "Yeah," matter-of-factly. Then she asked, "How did you do it?" When she said that, that is when my feminism began, right there, because I felt like crying. Because I did not realize how hard it had been to arrive at that apartment of my own and no one had understood how hard it was for me until Norma asked, "How did you do it?"

JH: How did you do it, stay single, considering the pressures from Mexican culture, the Church, and everyone else?

I had not realized how hard it had been, why I cried every weekend. I thought everyone cried every weekend. And I guess I did it because I had huevos! I had ganas because I knew I was not going to stay in my father's house. I had just come back from graduate school. I had tasted freedom and I liked it!

JH: What did freedom allow you to do?

I was able to travel for the first time in my life, independently to Europe. It was my first experience of living, traveling, and going off to exotic, interesting places and having adventures in meeting people. After that exciting year and a half, I came back to the place [the Midwest] where I began, and it was worse, now that I knew what was out there. I had been raised as a very traditional daughter and I was not allowed to go anywhere without my family, except graduate school. I was the kind of daughter who made trips to Mexico with the family. When I won a National Endowment for the Arts grant at twenty-eight, I took that money to live on the East Coast in Provincetown for a summer to finish *The House on Mango Street*. But I did not finish it on the East Coast. I took it with me to Europe, to Greece. I lived on an island, a very dramatic island, and finished the book there in the Aegean. Then I traveled through Paris and lived in the South of France. I moved all the way up and down Italy, ventured to Vienna, and wound up living in Sarajevo, where I have a close friend. Then I went back to Italy and Greece and came back with only a hundred bucks in my pocket. The last thing I wanted was to be stuck in the Midwest after I had traveled. I took the first job I applied for and got it. I just didn't want to be in Chicago. That job brought me to Texas. I was director of a literature program in a Chicano cultural arts center.

JH: How do you like living in San Antonio? Did it help you write *Woman Hollering Creek*?

Living in San Antonio gives me so much. It's so rich. There is so much to tap in terms of voices. There would be someone talking about soda water. What? Who says that? Nobody says soda water where I come from. I was listening for voices and stories, and I was gathering them up from all around me. There was a fear there, because I had to get the book done and I did not have a lot of money. I was really living in desperate circumstances so that I could use my advance for a longer time. There was this fever of writing as much as possible and getting the book done as soon as I could, just punching out the pages. I was also working on the sense of memory from my childhood that helped to create an invented Mexico, an imaginary Mexico, an imaginary homeland as Salman Rushdie would say.

BK: In this collection, what was your obsession at the time?

Woman Hollering Creek is very much set on the border because I am living at the border. I was much more concerned with representing different types of Chicanos on paper. I really felt my responsibility was to represent the entire spectrum of our community. But I did not want to write stories about people like myself because I was the exception. I felt a great responsibility to represent the community. I capture first voices I am most familiar with—the ones of people who go to the laundromat, the ones of girlfriends or my neighbors or my mother's voice. That is what I did with that one.

BK: I think "Eyes of Zapata" stands out as a historical piece in this collection.

In "Eyes of Zapata" I was obsessed with María Sabina and Emiliano Zapata. So I took my research and tried something new. I usually write about a woman obsessed with a man whom she makes into a God. I did the reverse this time: she made a legendary figure into a man. It was a great challenge for me to do that because I had to create a voice that was totally different from any of the other voices that I created. This voice was set in a different historical time, which, one would understand from the syntax, was speaking Spanish.

JH: You are also concerned with how women find themselves in love and relationships. At one point you say, "I am too romantic for marriage" in *Woman Hollering Creek*.

In "Never Marry a Mexican" the character is very unforgiving, which is why I gave her the name Clemencia. I really wanted to think about that aspect of myself. We are all these hybrids of emotions and feelings. So I took one aspect of myself, these demons. What is the meanest I have ever felt? I made that the basis. I wanted to write a modern-day Malinche story, not the historical Malinche as much as the mythological figure. How does the Malinche live in me? I took a lot of my women friends' situations or women I am related to who told me their stories. I always try to break stereotypes. I get so tired of Chicana writing glorifying mothers and grandmothers. So I decided to use a modern-day Malinche, but one who feels that the mother is too selfish or sacrificing. I always want to explore the things we are not supposed to.

JH: In modern times, I sense that the role of the bohemian artist in "Bien Pretty" has your spirit.

Well, when I got my Noah's ark of characters I realized that I had avoided any character that resembled me or anybody like me. But those characters are mainly the kind of people I hang out with. I realized that I had not indulged in a character like me. But I thought, well, I am valid, there are people like me. When I wrote that story I was really making a lot of fun of myself. I was really hard on the Lupe character who was so ridiculous, phony, and silly at first. When I started she was just a New Age, born-again Chicana. I like the story a lot. I was also reacting to two portrayals of Chicanas that had just come out, Alma Villanueva's *The Ultraviolet Sky* and Ana Castillo's *Sapogonia*. Who's paying for the rent on that loft? It seemed to me a romanticization and myth-making and overglorification of the Latina artist, not the reality. I knew about paying for an apartment in a scary neighborhood and pretending it was more romantic than poor.

BK: What is one of your major concerns with your community at this point?

As I am getting older, I am writing more about global connections. How do I make people understand that the war in Bosnia is affecting them? How does one connect with a massacre in Rwanda or a woman raped by pirates in the Asiatic Sea? How does one connect the killings of people in Chiapas to a worker here in San Antonio? What is my role as a writer to the citizens of this country? That is what I am concerned about currently. I also take my responsibility seriously of being a woman who lives on the border of cultures, a translator for a time when all these communities are shifting and colliding in history. Chicanos have that unique perspective.

JH: What is helping you grow spiritually?

Pain. When you ask for spiritual growth, you better believe it is some horrible pain that is going to happen in your life. It's always like when the shamans have their forty days in the desert. Horrible, horrible experiences that you are going through! But it is those horrible experiences that are going to take you to another level of spiritual awareness. I knew I needed them for the stories I had to tell, and then, of course, the most traumatic things in my life happened. My father is diagnosed with cancer and I watch him die. Someone very dear and close to me, a companion of the heart, disappears from my life. However horrible the events, you realize when they are happening, this is horrible, yet how lucky that I am a writer! I can muddle through. It's having a knife pulled out of your eye. There is a part of you that is in pain, but it is also fascinating to live through. I think writers are always split between living their life and watching themselves live it. It's the only way to live your life, or your life will kill you! I have to grow spiritually to be able to interpret and to guide. I find myself in the role of guiding a community.

BK: So painful experiences like death are an important part of life, especially to a writer. It is said that in Mayan culture, people don't die. They just live in another room.

Yes, I like how for the truly, truly, truly Mexican people, the dead are very present in their lives. That is not just a magic realism or quaint little New Age thing. It's true. You can't know it until it happens to you and you are initiated. Unless you lose someone you are very close to, you cannot know what other people are talking about. It connects you to humanity. I feel like I have been rowing a rowboat with a spoon. Since my father died, it has brought a lot of things into focus. I am living more intensely as a result of my father dying. I knew that when I started this book my father was going to die, and maybe some part of me was frightened because I almost felt that I had the power in the writing to make him die and I knew it was something I did not want to say. In the process of writing this book, I had to confront that reality. I had the potential of writing his death and, therefore, making him die. This is the book that is meant for me to write right now, to take me through this period of having to let my father go. The death of my father was just extraordinary. I think part of me knew that I could not finish the book until my father died, that there was some way that my father was going to help me write the book. He certainly has been there for me since his passing.

JH: Is your mother part of *Caramelo* [the novel]?

Not her story, but her voice. I like her voice. My mother's voice is the one of immigrant children who have had to fight for themselves in the streets of Chicago. She has helped me to create Latina characters who are very antistereotypical. I get so tired of seeing these religious fanatics.

My mother is very anti-Catholic. She is a freethinker, very bright, an amazing and extraordinary Latina woman. We know these amazing stories. There are women like her in our communities who think for themselves and cut out editorials instead of recipes, not formally educated but smart as could be and smart-mouthed. My mother had to be like that so my father could be soft and female. My mother was a very male woman. She had to be! Of course, she was not the popular parent. My father was. But she had her feet on the ground. She has a working-class Chicago voice that is the antithesis of my father's voice. My father is very much the lyrical voice in my writing, the child's voice in my writing. But that child's voice to me is so much part of our Mexicanness. It's so much part of our Mexican Spanish. Mexican Spanish is so childlike. The diminutives, the very tender, very sweet, very naive way of looking at nature. Its attitude toward the world is childlike and romantic. I don't mean childlike in the sense of being simple but meaning spiritual.

BK: What are you discovering in writing the novel?

I see so many things in the Mexican way of storytelling. It's a way of being nice to you even if it is a lie. For example, when I visit Mexico [City], I always go to the Basilica of the Virgen of Guadalupe. I go past the house that was my grandparents'. I always have a picture taken of myself in front of the recuerdo de Tepeyac backdrops. One day I explained to this gentleman, "Oh, my grandfather used to sell film to you, photographers, and the shop was right there." He asked, "Who was your grandfather? Oh, yes! I remember him." Of course, he did not remember him! But he had to tell me that story to make me feel good. As the daughter of a Mexican man, I knew that he was telling me a cuento. The Mexicans are cuentistas! They don't do this to deceive you or tell you bullshit. They do this because they want to give you a gift, a flower of a story. And my mother could never understand that, the difference between a story that someone gives to you and a lie. So I guess the most pivotal thing in my novel is telling stories, stories being told, people's versions of stories, whether something is puro cuento o cuento puro, all these layers of cuentos.

JH: Speaking of stories, which books provide a source of inspiration for you? What do you like to reread?

I like *The Ten Thousand Things* by María Dermout, a Dutch writer. I like to read *The Time of the Doves* by Mercé Rodoreda over and over. I like to read anything by Jean Rhys, especially her short stories. I like Marguerite Duras's *The Lover* as well as the sequel. I am also reading Carson McCullers over again. When I read her years ago, I was just reading her as a reader, whereas now I am reading her as a novelist. I am also reading Jane Austen again. I love reading almost any female or male author, but the women authors give me hope in my life. I think, how did this writer make this? When I read about the Brontës, for example, and the kind of lives they led and how hard it was for them, I think, wow! I am always concerned about the personal aspects of how an author finds time and money or spiritual substance to sustain oneself during the long, solitary voyage of creating.

JH: What is the special interest in the Catalan novelist, Mercé Rodoreda, for whom you wrote the foreword to her novel, *Camellia Street*?

I like Mercé Rodoreda because she is the writer I want to become, the writer I want to be. I guess we all have models that we want to follow, or combine the best of our favorites. She's my favorite writer. That is who I would like to write like. I think she does what I am trying to do. She does it in an extraordinary way. She does not have my sense of humor. She has the kind of breadth and scope that I can learn from. She has such a precise eye for detail and absolutely breathtaking passion and the ability to write sentences that are such a pleasure to read but move you emotionally. I want to move people at an emotional level. I want to write passages of such beautiful detail that they are a pleasure to read.

BK: If you could have dinner with a living writer whom you could never talk to again, who would it be?

I already had dinner with her, but I would do it again. I would love to spend more time with Dorothy Allison. She is just a phenomenal writer and very much a kind of sister in the work that we are doing for our communities, very parallel. I feel a kinship with her own fascination with sexual power and sexuality, creating stories of people who barely escape with their lives—survivors, a segment of the American population that has not been allowed to tell their stories. But, remember, we come from very different childhoods. She is a very busy writer whom I can't write or talk to as I would like because we are busy writing books. We don't disturb people when we are writing. But I feel uplifted when I read her work.

JH: My students feel very uplifted when they read your works. Do you see the importance of professors in academia who teach literature by Chicanos and Latinos?

Absolutely. Yes, absolutely, absolutely. That's exactly right.

JH: Are you teaching at all now?

Yes, I like where I am now. I volunteer when I feel like it. Since I don't get paid to teach, I can set the rules. It gives me an opportunity to have great fun at the Guadalupe Cultural Arts Center here in town where I used to work as a literary director.

JH: With that in mind, what advice do you have for a younger generation of writers?

I would encourage them to read everything, even other genres that they are not writing in. I would tell them to become very familiar with the other arts—painting, music—all the arts teach each other. I am very much uplifted by musicians, by Astor Piazzolla and the tango. That's who I want to write like, LIKE THAT! Maria Callas, the way she sings. Their hearts and souls move them. I see writers who are musicians or singers creating. I find them very inspirational, so I always want my younger students to look everywhere for that inspiration or for that level of excellence, writers who are aware of language. I think younger writers need to be very conscientious with their apprenticeship, because I think for so many becoming a writer means "publishing." And publishing is the least important level of verification because there is also a lot of shit out there that gets published! You do want to get published, but that should not be the only aim of writing. Writing is to get in touch with some intimate part of yourself. Publishing, fame, money, if you get it at all in your lifetime, is just icing on the cake but not the cake. Writing is a form of meditation.

(4)
A Side View

An Interview with Rosario Ferré

Rosario Ferré was born in Ponce, Puerto Rico, in 1938 and now lives in Condado, Puerto Rico. While finishing her B. A. at the University of Puerto Rico she started the literary magazine Zona de Carga y Descarga, *where some of her first stories were published. Ferré obtained her Ph.D. from the University of Maryland, where she worked with the Uruguayan critic Ángel Rama. She has held many visiting professorships, at Johns Hopkins University and the University of California at Berkeley, among other places. Ferré has published more than twenty books that reflect a wide range of interests and genres—novel, essay, short story, poetry, and literary criticism.*

I met Ferré on a Saturday afternoon at her home in Condado. She immediately offered me some mango juice and lunch. Her house was a cool haven from the heat, and we sat out on the porch. We exchanged pleasantries in both Spanish and English and, during a break, talked extensively in Spanish about island politics, ranging from the University of Puerto Rico to being Puerto Rican on the island versus on the mainland. When the tape recorder was on, Ferré was not as interested in speaking of her writing rituals as in her evolution as a writer, where she has come from and where she is headed. This seems to be a period of reflection for her and of great emotion with regard to her family and her history. She consciously wrote her novel Eccentric Neighborhoods *(1997) in response to the family stories told to her by both her parents. The emotion, and some of the Spanish, seeped into the second half of the interview. She understands her motivation for writing, and of all the writers interviewed, she is the most self-critical. Her best book, she said at one point, is yet to come.*

Ferré has always provoked controversy on the island. While her father, Luis A. Ferré, was governor and promoted statehood, she remained a radical pro-independence activist. However, she recently declared her support of statehood for the island, which, needless to say, created a furor. With the publication of her novels in English, Ferré proved herself to be a truly bilingual writer. But rather than arouse admiration, her work in English provoked accusations of betrayal from politicians, critics, and the public. Ironically, the accusations reflect the power and importance of her voice on the island. Despite everything, people follow her every move and read every word she writes. This can be a blessing, but it can also be a curse. Our discussion begins with the coming and going of contemporary Caribbean writers, the juggling of the ever-closer two worlds.

B.K.

BK: Do you see the literary Caribbean as more integrated with the United States than other parts of the continent?

Definitely. A new literary boom vox is playing in the Caribbean that is very audible in the United States today. The previous literary explosion was a continental phenomenon. Vargas Llosa, García Márquez, Donoso, Allende—they were all from the mainland. But many of the Hispanic writers doing interesting things now are from the archipelago: Cuba, the Dominican Republic, Puerto Rico. A number of them are women born on the islands, others are daughters of women who were born there. Take the Cubans like Cristina García, Wendy Gimbel, Mayra Montero, for example, as well as the Puerto Ricans Irene Vilar, Ana Lydia Vega, Judith Ortiz Cofer, and Esmeralda Santiago and the Dominican Julia Alvarez. They are all writing interesting novels.

BK: I'd like to refer specifically to your essay "On Translation," which you subtitled "Ophelia Adrift on the C. and O. Canal." Why did you title it that way? Does the suspension of reality that you believe necessary to literature imply an enriching but also a painful experience for you?

All writing is, in essence, a translation of reality into imagination. Writing implies a passage, a transformation that brings echoes of death and rebirth. This is why I see it as a suicidal activity. To pass into what you are becoming, you have to die to what you are. This was the reason I used Ophelia in the title of my essay "On Translation." Ophelia threw herself into the river because she believed Hamlet no longer loved her, and for a few minutes she floated on the surface, buoyed by her billowing robes. As she did so, she sang a beautiful song that moves me as no other passage in Shakespeare does. For a few seconds love and death meant nothing, Ophelia couldn't be hurt by them because she was protected by her song. This is the role of literature.

BK: What moves you to write? Cortázar, one of your favorite authors, describes it as the alimaña, the beast. How would you describe the experience?

I think you bring to writing a lot of baggage from childhood. Certain things are there for years, as if they were sitting inside a closet, waiting. And then one day they come out of the dark and you either take them apart or they fly at you. Why do they turn on you at a certain time and not at others? I have no idea.

BK: Borges said once that to be a writer is to be a daydreamer, to be living a double life. Is that true for you?

Probably. For example, I like to be with my husband and not talk. It bothers me when people need to talk all the time. It's as if they have to make sure they are not alone. I remember that, when I was young, people talked less. They were shy, and there was a fear of sounding ridiculous that has totally disappeared. This is both good and bad. On the one hand, we've become exhibitionists. It gives us a charge to hang out our dirty laundry for everyone to see, to scandalize our neighbor. But I think this also has to do with defiance, with our struggle against repression and our need to tell the truth. We come from a world where discipline and repression were very present—in Victorian England as well as in Spain and the rest of Europe. Society had to be structured in order not to succumb to natural disasters, or to social threats like those of Hitler and fascism. Today, fortunately, this has changed. We live in much more flexible societies, but we have to keep testing them, pushing against the lid of the system so it doesn't crush us again. And one of the best ways to do this is to be frank about one's own experiences.

BK: Do your writing ideas come from daydreaming?

An idea can come from anywhere. For example, when Hurricane Hugo passed through Puerto Rico, the oak tree in my backyard was left bare as a piece of flotsam. A few weeks later it flowered out of season. I identified with the oak and wrote a poem about it, because disaster has at times served to make me write.

BK: Can you remember some of the books that have influenced you as a writer, or that made you want to be a writer?

When I first read *Wuthering Heights* I was ten years old and I loved it. I discovered that people in faraway places could be as passionate as those around me. Cathy Heathcliff was my first literary role model. Then I read *Jane Eyre* and didn't like it half as much. Jane was too rational and well behaved, but I admired her stamina. She had grace under pressure, something I've always respected. I've also read Cervantes's *El Quixote* several times, and Faulkner's *As I Lay Dying*. Those four authors, Emily and Charlotte Brontë, Cervantes, and Faulkner are some of the ones I remember more often, but I can't tell if they have influenced me more than others.

BK: If you could spend one evening with a writer, who would it be and why?

I don't think I'd like to spend it with a male writer because men don't like to talk to women about their work. I'd love to spend it with a female writer, Joyce Carol Oates, for example, or Ana Castillo. Ana is not only a wonderful writer, she exudes an assurance that's contagious; when I'm near her I feel, Hey! Writing about our world is important. We can help each other. She makes me feel good. Other times she reminds me of the sacredness of writing, that it's a vocation, something I usually try to hide. Because I live surrounded by everyday people, when someone mentions I'm a writer or asks me about my next book, I usually laugh, shrug, make a face or cross my eyes like a clown, and tell them scribbling words is just a hobby I practice when I get bored sitting at home. People feel threatened by writers; they often see them as candid cameras that might pull a trick on them at any moment. And it's true, writers, like scientists, must find the data for their experiments by observing what's going on around them. But writing has to be a very serious commitment in order for it to be any good.

BK: Do you write all the time? Which genre is hardest for you to write?

Since I wrote my first book, *Papeles de Pandora*, twenty-eight years ago, I've written 20 books, 16 in Spanish and 4 in English, and have always practiced some kind of journalism. When I was thirteen years old my grandfather gave me a diary as a present, and I discovered I had an ability with words. I was terrible with numbers and almost flunked math, but words came easily to me.

I began jotting down my observations in my diary. My first entry was about my grandfather, who was always being scolded by my grandmother for feeding his German shepherds at the table. It was the first time I realized two people could be right about the same thing, in spite of diverging opinions. My grandmother thought it was unsanitary to feed the dogs at the table because they had tics and fleas that might land in our food. But it made my grandfather happy. Since I couldn't make up my mind about who was right, I tried to make the description of the process of dogs snapping at flying chicken bones as objective as possible.

Writing is about touching people's hearts—in Spanish we say "conmover," which literally means to move *with* the reader, to make the other feel. We move our bodies when we're making love, and I've always thought about writing as a way to make love: you give and receive understanding, compassion, support, advice, knowledge, and pleasure. Without communication there is no love. This is the commitment a writer has to literature.

I've written short stories, poems, and novels, and I find the novel the most difficult genre. Not only because the techniques are more complicated, but because it demands a longer expanse of time. To come up with the structure of a novel you have to think about it for a long time. It doesn't just appear by magic. A poem or a short story is easier because it is shorter and self-contained.

Three of my novels, *Maldito amor, La casa de la laguna,* and *Vecindarios eccéntricos,* have taken four years each to write. A seven-page short story usually takes two months, and I may do ten versions of it. With a poem it's the same. I usually write a first draft, then put it away so that it cools down and grows away from me. I get a funny feeling during this time that the poem or short story has a will of its own. As the days pass and I don't look at the manuscript, the poem or short story thinks I've forgotten it, and so it does what it wants. It becomes self-satisfied, and all the defects come out. Then I go back, pick out all the defects, and edit them.

In a novel you have to extend your concentration. The longer the text, the harder it is to write—like staying underwater for a long time. You can't come up to breathe, because the minute you do, you'll lose your momentum and forget what happened six or seven chapters before. The emotions need to be kept at a pitch. The novelist is like a long-distance runner; he has to develop the stamina to keep going, even when he's afraid that what he's writing is trash. And it very well might be, because a novel is made up of good and bad writing. A writer can't approach every subject with the same insight or passion, because his or her experience is limited. But if the novel as a whole succeeds, then those imperfect or boring passages blend in with the rest and you can hardly tell which are the bad ones.

BK: Was *La casa de la laguna* a breakthrough for you, as your first long novel?

That might be true. I couldn't have written it if I hadn't written *Papeles de Pandora* and two shorter novels, *Maldito amor* and *La batalla de las vírgenes,* before it. With each book I gained a little more stamina, I pushed myself to write a longer text.

BK: You have always done your own translations, both Spanish to English and English to Spanish. Why do you choose to do your own translations?

I don't translate my work; I write versions of it. I couldn't let anybody do it for me. We're a different self in each language, since language makes you think in different ways. I feel if I let someone else translate my work, the translator would stamp his personality on it. The translator speaks with your voice, but the soul behind the voice is someone else's. The relationship between the writer and his or her translator is a little like that between identical twins. They are born with the same features, but because each soul is different, the facial expression alters the body's configuration; identical twins end up looking very different when they are older.

Of course, the matter of translation is out of a writer's control most of the time. We have to put ourselves in the translator's hands and let him redo us at will. A good translator gets inside the soul of the writer.

BK: Language seems to be one of your central themes; it preoccupies you.

Yes, language is one of my central themes. Not any particular language, English or Spanish, but language as an instrument of art. Like Isabel in *La casa de la laguna*, I've been trying to become a writer for many years. A writer is not something you can be and remain so for the rest of your life. You can learn the craft. There are techniques of how to write a poem, a novel, a short story. But writing also needs inspiration. Some things *inspire* us—bring us into the wind—and others don't. And we never know for sure what those things are going to be, although we may suspect some. That's why we keep a closet full of strange objects and memories in mind, in the hope that, when we approach a literary theme and bring them out, they'll confer on it that magic glow. But since we can never be sure what the results will be, we must become writers every day.

Writers are artisans to begin with; and in that sense we belong to another age. We create products that are crafted word by word, with excruciating slowness. From the point of view of the writer, even if a novel is mass produced, once it's finished, the work that has gone into it is unique, it cannot be reproduced even by the author. Once the words are down, the moment passes. The author is not the same person, her life is completely different and she could never write the same novel again.

Something similar happens with music. A Mozart concerto is the same in every musical score, but it's interpretation will vary. The concert player plays it his way and the listener understands it another; there are two barriers to be overcome in order for Mozart's musical intentions to reach the audience. But words are more porous than musical notes, which are controlled by the law of mathematics. They become permeated by the reader's emotions at every step, even after they appear on the printed page. Words are vulnerable to the reader in a way music is never vulnerable to the listener, because meaning is like a malleable paste. As in music, intonation, inflection, and speed all have an effect on them. But they are also altered by the experience of the reader, which is ever changing. A literary text is never the same, even when it's read by the same person twice.

BK: Why the title *La casa de la laguna?*

The title refers to the fact that the Mendizabals's house is built on a mangrove swamp, which is halfway territory: half earth, half water. The crustaceans that live in the mangrove are amphibians; they can live on earth and water. And Puerto Rico is a lot like that, it's a borderline country. Puerto Ricans are a hybrid people: Hispanic and American, part Caribbean Indian and part African, and many other things. We speak both Spanish and English; are born to Spanish culture, which is enormously rich; and have, by necessity, acquired many American traits. This ambivalence has been our problem because it's very hard to be two things at the same time. Nationalism is a much more accessible attitude: you are one thing only and defend yourself against the invasion of "the other." In addition to this, Spanish culture and English culture have been enemies for centuries. They represent two opposite visions of the world. One is spiritual and mystical, with its roots in Catholicism, which defines existence in terms of a specific doctrine: you are either good or bad, saved or damned. The other is pragmatic, mercantile and positivist, rooted in Protestantism and individualism: you make up your doctrine, confess your sins only to yourself. Nationalism as an ideal inspired most Latin American countries during the nineteenth and twentieth centuries and led its leaders to do great things. But in Puerto Rico the formula doesn't work anymore. The twenty-first century is going to be much more complex, and nationalism must be approached from a different angle. Puerto Ricans are already experiencing these changes. We have had to develop a chameleon nature to cope with our complex circumstances. This chameleon nature, the necessity to blend in with different visions of life, implies the fact that there is not one truth but many. We've had to arrive at this conclusion to live with ourselves.

BK: How do you explain the whole theme that emerges from *La casa de la laguna* regarding fiction versus history?

The theme of the novel is the relativity of all truth, which often entails a struggle between emotion and reason. Fiction, which is Isabel's turf since she's the one writing the novel, refers to the emotional history of her family (and of her country, Puerto Rico). To write fiction you don't just see and hear what reality is like, you have to experience it. History, Quintín's turf, is always rational; it narrates a verifiable sequence of events that took place in the past. The end of the novel is a victory for fiction and for Isabel, since it's her version of the story that prevails. Quintín loses, not because he was right or wrong—we never know if what Isabel wrote in her novel was true, or whether he was the victim instead of her—but because he couldn't move us as Isabel did, because he didn't write well enough to make us believe him. The novel underlines the power of fiction, of heart over mind.

BK: There's a marked change between your earlier work and what you've written in the nineties, which seems more autobiographical. Is this true?

Everything I write is autobiographical, but the events in my books are fiction. They are made up. When I write a novel, the skeleton—the main story line—may run parallel to some event in my life. But the flesh that fills it in is fiction.

BK: The mother-daughter relationship is very moving in *Vecindarios eccéntricos*. Is this based on your own experience?

Vecindarios eccéntricos revolved around Elvira's search for her dead mother. But this relationship is only examined at the end; there are a number of stories that are narrated first. My relationship with my mother, like Elvira's in the book, was difficult. This is probably why the book took so long to write: I had an original manuscript in Spanish that I wrote ten years ago and eventually discarded. When my father turned ninety—four years ago—I realized it was very important to finish the novel. I wanted him to read it before he passed away, so that maybe we could talk about things we had never dared bring up. He was the third person I had to read the novel to, after my agent and my editor.

BK: What about the title, *Vecindarios eccéntricos*? Why did you choose it to represent the two families?

The word "eccentric" in Spanish has two meanings: strange, unusual; but also off-center. I see Puerto Rico as a border, a place where everyone wants to go someplace else. Puerto Ricans have always traveled a lot. An island gets on your nerves after a while and you become claustrophobic. But it doesn't matter how far you travel, there's a good probability you'll find a Puerto Rican living there, dreaming of going back home. Today we have immigrants from Cuba, Santo Domingo, and Haiti on the island; many of them are illegal. They see us as a stepping-stone in their voyage to the United States. There is literally a very *volatile* sense of national identity, which determines our character as a nation.

BK: Do you read contemporary Latina writers? What would you say is the Latina writer's most important contribution?

I've read Cristina García's two novels, which I liked. Cuba and Puerto Rico have a lot in common, even after the transformations Cuba has gone through. I also like Ana Castillo, Sandra Cisneros, Julia Alvarez, Denise Chávez, Cristina Benítez, Pat Mora . . . there are so many of them! I think Latina writers today, even more than Latino writers, are trying to integrate both cultures, the Hispanic and the Anglo. There is a conscious effort to include both visions, like V. S. Naipaul does in his novels: the native and the foreign, the colonizers and the colonized. There's an effort to underline the importance of the "side view" in them, of the border town. From the border you have access to more roads, and the perspective—front and back—can be 180 degrees. Spanish and English, those two opposing paths that have kept the New World divided for centuries, are beginning to merge at last into a third path.

That's what these new novels are really about: a new United States, where half of the population will be Latino in the next century.

(5)

At Home on the Page

An Interview with Cristina García

Our first interview with Cristina García was conducted at Borders book-store in Los Angeles on June 7, 1996. It continued in her home in Los Ange-les more than a year later, in December 1997. At our first interview García requested that no tape recorders be used. She felt self-conscious and believed that the best interviews are those that are handwritten. In her opinion they capture the essence of the conversation and are not as boring and contrived. This is the only interview for which we took notes. García is extremely per-sonable and outspoken, especially regarding Cuba, Miami, and Cuba's ac-claimed hero, José Martí, who she believes "is so overrated." García's work presents a complicated picture of what it means to be Cuban in the United States and adds a refreshing dimension to the Cuban literature being writ-ten here. One of the most important themes that García wishes to convey to her audience is that there is no one Cuban exile. Perhaps because she is more open to what being American and Cuban means, García has an uncom-fortable relationship with Cuba and its community, both in Miami and on the island. She spent a year and a half in Miami while working for Time, *and has returned there on different occasions yet has never felt part of that community.*

García was born in Havana, Cuba, in 1958. Her family left Cuba in 1961 for political reasons, and she grew up in Brooklyn, New York. García was *an undergraduate at Barnard College and then went to Johns Hopkins University where she received an M. A. in international studies. She worked as a* Time *correspondent for several years in New York, San Francisco, Miami, and Los Angeles. She currently lives with her daughter, Pilar, in California. García's first novel,* Dreaming in Cuban *(1992), for which she was a finalist for the 1992 National Book Award, traces three generations of Cuban women and explores how the revolution "rearranged" their lives. Her next novel,* The Agüero Sisters *(1997), focuses on Cuban history from a different angle. The main theme is the relationship between two sisters and how they come to terms with their past, a past based on lies. As García bluntly says, "I wanted to explore all the lying that goes on in Cuban history." She also has published an illustrated documentary book called* Cars of Cuba *(1995) and several anthologized short stories, for example, "Inés in the Kitchen," collected in* Little Havana Blues, *and "Tito's Goodbye," which appears in* Iguana Dreams.*

Our interview began with a discussion of Miami and Cuba. Miami is seen as the home-away-from-home for the Cuban community. In this respect, it dictates the political opinions, social mores, and even identity for Cubans in the United States. According to García, Miami has created a hierarchy of identities for Cubans in the United States, and she falls into the last tier, that of "other Cubans."

B.K.

BK: What is your present relationship to Cuba and Miami?

In general, my family in the United States is frothing-at-the-mouth anti-Castro. I'm not so much, but I do think enough already! of Fidel Castro. As a child I used to listen to accounts of family history from my mother. But then, when I first went back to Cuba, in 1984, I developed a strong relationship with my grandmother and realized how distorted those accounts from my mother were, how nostalgia and anger had clouded her version of events. My mother's family is still in Cuba and lives in Guanabo and in Havana. Before 1984 I did not have any contact with my family in Cuba. My daughter, who is five, has already been to Cuba three times. I take her so that she knows she is part Cuban, so that she has a sense of being Cuban, of Cuba and of her family roots.

My relationship with Miami Cubans is often uncomfortable. Miami is such a political hothouse that suffers little dissidence. It can be an intolerant place. It is frequently monolithic in its approach to Cuba. As far as Cuban identity goes, there are three concentric circles—the Cubans, the Miami-Cubans, and the other Cubans. I'm in the third ring three times removed!

BK: You said that when you first lived in Miami you felt alienated.

That's absolutely true. I still have a love-hate relationship with Miami. I suffer from my own distorted nostalgia, because though I always look forward to going to Miami, thirty-six hours after I land there I get depressed. I can almost set my watch by that onset of depression. It is always this sense of looking forward to going and feeling like I'm going to belong. I don't know why that is, because every time I go, I don't belong. But there is always the hope of feeling at one with the place. It never happens. I feel that to write about the Cuban experience I probably have to be, in some ways, as far away from it as possible.

JH: Could you tell us about your Barnard days? What did you gain from that experience?

I was largely unconscious about what I was doing when I was at Barnard. I was on this self-imposed accelerated program to graduate. I only took one English class the whole time I was there, but it was this course, on the novella, that got me onto a reading campaign that has never stopped. I was a voracious reader as a kid, but I lost it in my teens because I worked in my parents' retail business and restaurant all the time. There was virtually no time to read. I would say that the greatest gift from Barnard was opening the door to reading again. My first assignment was Kafka's *Metamorphosis*. You can imagine. By then I was already accepted into graduate school at Johns Hopkins in political science. But I spent my two years in graduate school reading literature. I barely made it out of graduate school.

JH: After studying at Johns Hopkins, you headed into journalism. Why did you choose this career?

I think temperamentally journalism suited me much better than being a novelist. For me there is nothing more fun than landing in a strange city and finding out what is going on and making my way. I remember once being in Salt Lake City just before Christmas. The whole place was lit up, and I saw families with seven children all in a row walking down the street, and I thought, what planet have I landed on! I just loved it. The adrenaline rush of going someplace at the last minute, packing an extra change of clothes, and getting on a plane. I had the opportunity to dip into so many different lives I normally would have no access to. One day I could be talking with computer people in Silicon Valley, and the next I could be visiting some hog ranch in Nevada.

JH: How did your training in journalism help you as a prose fiction writer?

It was good training in terms of developing my eye for detail and, since I worked for a weekly magazine, for picking up things that the rest of the pack didn't have the luxury to do.

BK: Speaking of details, I was fascinated by your story "Inés in the Kitchen" that appears in *Little Havana Blues*. Tell me about the history of this short story, is it your first?

I harvested the story from a dead novel. I felt like a necrophiliac going back and plucking it from the deadness. I think in some ways I was writing about my own stifled feelings in my marriage. But it was also about what I saw around me, cousins of mine getting married, moving to the suburbs, having, as that old phrase goes, quietly desperate lives. A cousin of mine once told me, referring to her husband, "If I had ten thousand dollars I would leave him," and I thought, that is what it would take?! Personally, I was very happy to be pregnant, very ready, but I think it takes a toll on you and really divides your life. For me the great divide of humanity is people with children and people without. But I don't really consider myself a short story writer by nature.

JH: What's the difference between a novel and a short story for you?

For me novels are so huge and forgiving. You can funnel everything into them. They are looser, whereas the constraints and exactitudes of a short story are more difficult for me. Generally, things spin out of control. For example, with a novel it can initially start out as an idea for a short story, but then the roots start growing together and it begins evolving into a longer work.

BK: Can you describe your ritual of writing? García Márquez once remarked that he wrote from 6:00 a.m. until noon uninterrupted, which is difficult as a mother. How do you find the time and space?

I have a ritual, and it must be inviolate. My solution was to get an office outside of the house. This I did when my daughter was eighteen months old. My office space is my sanctuary. When I have momentum going, I work for about five or six hours Monday through Friday. I don't have a telephone there. And my daughter is in school now so it's easier. Of those five or six hours, I have to spend two hours reading, mostly poetry, as a transition into the writing. Otherwise I might still be humming the Winnie the Pooh theme song.

BK: Do you start out with an outline, characters, or themes?

I tried working with an outline for the dead novel. So you see what happened to that! There was no discovery along the way. Now I just sort of buckle my seatbelt and see what happens. For example, I don't really know what this new novel is about, it is still evolving. I only started writing it in September [1997], and I am quite surprised at the events that are unfolding. I never expected to be in some of these places, like Shanghai in 1939. And even the way I am writing it is very different. I hope I can pull it off or I may have to get a real job.

Writing is very language driven for me. I spend a lot of time reading poetry in my office and seeing what catches, what phrase or what images begin to congeal and what the departure point for that day's work will be. I read as broadly as possible, often around what I am writing at the time. I read a great deal of history, biography, memoirs, that sort of thing, not too many novels. But mostly what I read is poetry. On any given day I could be reading classical Chinese poetry in translation side by side with Adrienne Rich or Octavio Paz. And everything in between.

BK: What about José Martí, a leader in Cuba's struggle for independence but also a well-known poet? Did you ever read him for inspiration?

I've read a lot of his poetry and a little about his life and so on, but to be honest—and I think this will be sacrilegious—he is so overrated. In the Cuban context, everybody claims him for himself. The beginning of pretty much every Cuban text, whether by Fidel Castro or the Cuban American National Foundation, quotes José Martí. Everyone wants a piece of him.

JH: What authors have influenced your writing or served as mentors?

My mentors were all the writers I had read up until the time I started writing, when I was about thirty. *Anna Karenina, Madame Bovary.* Anything by Virginia Woolf. I was primarily a reader, and I think the reading is what led me to writing. I was always drawn to contemporary writers like Toni Morrison, Louise Erdrich, and Maxine Hong Kingston. Their relative "outsider" positions help make them exceedingly powerful observers. Yet the earlier works by many "other" writers were more sociological. (I can just see the lynch mob coming at me for this one!) Now the literature is truly artistic, much more poetic. As more Latinos are born and raised here, it improves their overall educational base. That, combined with not being strictly part of the mainstream, is producing exciting literature.

It's strange, but I came to Latin American literature last. First I read Tolstoy, Flaubert, Woolf. It wasn't until my twenties that I started to read the Latin American writers. They sparked my imagination and I've read all the Latino authors. I read everything Sandra Cisneros writes.

BK: What's so exciting about Latina literature for you?

These fascinating stories, traditionally on the margin, are redefining American literature. Broadening, muscling in, and expanding on what is considered serious American literature. Before it was relegated to the margins or to the sociology shelf, and now, after some time, the writing has just gotten too good to ignore.

JH: You have commented on Sandra Cisneros's *Loose Woman.* Could you elaborate further?

Yes, of course. I thought the poems were very audacious, and sexy, and laugh-out-loud funny. There was a kind of mock-serious tone to them, and I found them extremely entertaining. They made me want to know her, to belt back a few tequilas with her, and I hardly even drink!

BK: Can we move on to your works and what your protagonists mean to you? In our first interview you said that Pilar from *Dreaming in Cuban* was your alter ego. You've also said that in relation to Reina and Constancia, the protagonists of *The Agüero Sisters*. Where do you fit in between all these alter egos—Cuba, language, and self?

I'm not sure that I know myself. I could say that they are my alter egos, but I could also say that I am made up of alter egos. [Laughs] Maybe I am, at the center, blanca, blank! How pathetic! [Laughs] The truth is they are all parts of me. Maybe alter ego is not quite accurate. I think I identify to some degree with everyone, from Pilar Puente and her punctured Statue of Liberty painting to the worst excesses of Lourdes and even Heberto from *The Agüero Sisters*. I think there is something of me in all of them.

The thing I hate most in the Cuban context is this attempt to limit what it means to be Cuban. Not too long ago at a reading I gave in Puerto Rico, a man stood up and said, "You can't be Cuban because you write in English." The point for me is that there is no one Cuban exile. I am out here in California and may not fit in anywhere, but I am Cuban too. I think I am trying to stake out a broader territory. There is a weird cultural balkanization going on in this country that I recoil from. For me, the emphasis should be on amplitude and inclusion.

BK: What about the categorization of ethnic literatures?

I don't think that literature should be demographically or politically representative. You can't do that to literature. But I do respect the different ethnic territories, because one has to respect different traditions and forms. I think there are very distinct differences historically in terms of tradition and migration that in some ways quite radically alter one's perspective. But since I have only become a "professional Cuban" in the last few years it is all very amusing to me, and puzzling too. I joke with my friends and say, "I'm going to go do my professional Cuban thing now." That's what it feels like sometimes, and there are certain bizarre expectations that can go along with it.

BK: What are some of those expectations?

The presumption that I'm trying to speak for the whole Cuban experience. For me, the Cuban community is an evolving culture with many different influences. I feel that there is a lot more diversity in Miami now than there used to be. I find it a much more open and porous place than when I was living there in the mid-1980s. What I try to emphasize are the particularities of my characters, the specificities of their obsessions. I'm not trying to create models or types or prototypes or archetypes. I'm trying to create complicated characters with smooth surfaces. I work these surfaces, interior and exterior, to make them come alive. Even though there is something about them that can be distilled as Cuban, I would be disappointed if it began and ended there, if people from other cultures couldn't relate to or see themselves in my characters.

JH: And your first work, *Dreaming in Cuban*, deals with a variety of characters that all have different relationships to Cuba and the United States. Could you comment on the dream motif both in the title and in the work?

I'm afraid that I can't take credit for the title. It was not my idea. My agent came up with it. Originally it was called "Tropics of Resemblances" from the Wallace Stevens poem, but nobody could remember it or knew what the hell it meant. I actually thought it was a very good title, and appropriate for this work, since each character in the book projects her own version of Cuba. For each one of them, the revolution is the great dividing factor in their lives. Whole families get rearranged by it. I felt that I was trying to look at Cuba in the round. For me, it was not black and white. I'm presenting different points of view that I don't think can be categorized in the official polarization that exists in the Cuban context. Literarily, I'm trying to complicate the picture because it is extremely complicated. I think many believe that complications dilute clarity, but I couldn't disagree more. I think it is just the opposite. The more you can encompass the complexity of a situation, the closer to the truth you get, not the other way around.

JH: Contemporary Latin American authors have been important in the development of your works. Take Gabriel García Márquez.

I was reading him assiduously when I was writing *Dreaming in Cuban*. I think he's part of the water table for all Latino or Latina writers. He just informs everything. In some way he seeps into every sentence. The total license he gives to the imagination is unparalleled. For me, he was a discovery, a liberation.

JH: You have also mentioned Borges and Vargas Llosa. Why?

I remember reading something in the *Paris Review* by Vargas Llosa where he says that Borges is the only Latin American writer who has as many ideas as words. I admire Borges's brilliance, his concision. His erudition. Every word opens doors. Like Chekhov's short stories. I turn to them again and again for solace and inspiration.

With Vargas Llosa it is a different story. When I was a reporter, I followed him on the campaign trail. It was so bizarre to see him in small villages in the Amazon trying to convince the locals to vote for him. Bizarre and surreal. I like some of his novels, but others are impenetrable to me. I certainly didn't like him as a politician. His *Fish Out of Water* was good when it discussed his memoirs, his relationship with his father, but awful and petty in the political parts. It was a litany of keeping score.

But now, like I said, I read poetry more. I revere Wallace Stevens. He was the first poet to truly dazzle me. For me, poetry fuels the imagination. Poetry is driven by a different logic than novels, it resists deconstruction. If you don't understand the poem, you can still allow yourself to be awash in the language.

JH: Why did you decide to incorporate Spanish in your work? What was the goal?

My use of Spanish is very conscious and judicious. I remember my agent first saying that she didn't understand it all. But I felt very strongly that what was in Spanish should remain in Spanish. If people were interested enough, they could pick up a damn dictionary! When I am reading books and there are words in a foreign language I either get it from the context or I look it up. Some things I think would just be diminished by translation. In a way my writing in English is an act of translation anyway.

BK: Why is writing in English an act of translation for you?

Well, I think most of what I am writing about would normally be taking place in Spanish. Yet here I am writing it in English, approximating it in English, trying to rework the English to sound more like Spanish.

BK: What is the element that pushes you to include Spanish?

There's a kind of musicality and cadence in Spanish that works its way into my English. When I read the Spanish translation of *The Agüero Sisters* it felt like more of a restoration than a translation. Talk about an identity crisis! But I think a lot of immigrant literatures are making English do things it hasn't done before. These other languages and cultures are pushing English to do new things. I think these new borderlands of language are where it's happening.

BK: One of the complexities of all these Spanish-speaking communities is what happens to the language. There's a lot of debate about Spanglish, or as Pérez-Firmat calls it, nilingue, neither Spanish nor English. Could you comment on the use of Spanglish, code switching, as a verbal and written form of communication?

I don't consider myself entirely fluent in Spanish. In fact, it would be impossible for me to do this interview in Spanish, because I feel that I don't have any kind of subtlety in Spanish. I am frustrated and embarrassed by that Spanish. And yet at the same time I don't feel that I should be judged by my lack of perfect Spanish. It is very hard to be a Rosario Ferré, truly bilingual. I know very few people who are fully bilingual. There is always one language that is more dominant. I came here when I was two years old, and I was educated here and studied numerous other languages. Perhaps if I were to dedicate the next two or three years to reading only in Spanish I could probably speak it better. But what are the trade-offs? I don't know. I do know that it is important for me that my daughter speak Spanish or be exposed to Spanish, and she is. I feel like I wouldn't know half of what goes on in California if I didn't know Spanish. The fact that it is not at the level of my English, I mean, give me a break.

BK: Do you feel that languages should be pure, without any inflections or "infections" of the other language?

That is so artificial. Languages are continually influencing each other. When *The Agüero Sisters* got to Spain the people there were totally disdainful of the Spanish in the book. They called it substandard Spanish because it was very Caribbean. They were saying this is not castellano. Well, damn right it is not castellano. I got into a big row with them about it. This kind of snobbery and linguistic colonialism exists, but I'm pretty dismissive of it. I think new hybrids are being formed all the time. I am very interested in what happens to language as a result.

BK: How did you do research for *The Agüero Sisters,* and what inspired the natural history background as a point of departure?

I think it was a way of trying to get at Cuban history without necessarily focusing on the watershed of the revolution. B.R./A.R., before revolution and after revolution. I wanted a different landscape and scope. I wasn't fully conscious of this ahead of time. But I wanted to get away from the gravitational pull of the revolution and look at loss and memory and nostalgia and extinction and myth making through another prism. I wanted a different kind of metaphor. I think the natural history theme was useful that way. I also wanted to explore all the lying that goes on in Cuban history, to put it bluntly.

BK: And that is the opening to your novel, the telling of seventeen years of lies, which creates all the conflict and haunts the daughters throughout the plot.

Yes. And they each take sides. The Cuban community is a very polarized community. No matter where you stand it is either you are with me or you are against me. It is very black and white. Or it can be. Again, it is changing. So there was something there too that I wanted to explore, but again I didn't want it revolving strictly around the revolution. I started researching the details of Cuba's natural history when I was living in Hawaii, which is where I finished *Dreaming in Cuban*. I had a little cottage on the edge of a swamp. What I didn't know was that it was a migratory paradise for wintering birds from Alaska. I ended up getting binoculars and a little inflatable canoe and was up in the mornings checking out the birds. Believe me, this was very strange for me, having grown up in New York and barely being able to discern the difference between a pigeon and a squirrel! The University of Hawaii also had a wonderful collection of old travel diaries on Cuba as well as naturalists' accounts of their experiences on the island. And so I began keeping tabs on the Alaskan ducks and researching.

BK: The other interesting aspect of this book is the explicit exhaustion and impatience that some characters have with the revolution. For example, Reina's daughter Dulce.

I think this is the mood in Cuba. It wasn't when I first went to Cuba in 1984, but when I went back again in 1995, right in the wake of the *Período Especial,** people had had it. I mean, one aunt of mine was selling underwear just to get food on the table. It was really bad and everyone had lost weight. It was stressful. I had seen my cousins trying to leave the country any which way. Everyone was cornering me trying to figure out if I could write them invitations on university letterhead. I got marriage proposals. I mean, anything to get out of the country.

BK: Your characters renounce the revolution in many ways. Did you receive any negative criticism for your portrayal of the revolution?

Well I don't think it is a 100 percent renunciation. I think Reina [one of the protagonists in the novel] probably best represents this attitude in that she is glad to leave Cuba but she also doesn't want the exiles defining or defiling it. The only really negative reaction I got was from this one woman who thought I was much too harsh on the Miami Cubans, that I was making fun of them and ridiculing them. I haven't received any official or nonofficial response from Cubans on the island. But I would be curious to know. Cuba is so much of a fictitious world in a way. I remember this one actress who was in *Strawberries & Chocolate* told me that it was very clear that I had never lived on the island. I don't think she was trying to be insulting. But she felt that my work had nothing to do with the Cuba she knew. And Pilar Puente in *Dreaming in Cuban* said, "There is only our imagination where our history should be." And

*The "Special Period" began in October 1990. As Cuba struggled economically from the withdrawal of Russian aid, Castro announced that Cuba had entered a "special period in time of peace." It meant stricter rations on food, fuel, and electricity.

that is exactly my situation, I think. For me, Cuba is as much about imagining and projection and perception as truth and history.

BK: Can we return to your childhood and what it was like growing up in Brooklyn?

I was a Jewish New Yorker before I was Cuban. I wasn't a rebel like Pilar in *Dreaming in Cuban*. My mother would have killed me.

JH: You once said that your mother inspired your spirit in life. Did she help you achieve your goals?

She would love me to say yes to that. Maybe I should. [Laughs] I am fascinated with the mother-daughter relationship, especially now that I have a daughter myself. My mother is a very wonderful, complicated woman. I still won't get in a taxi with her because I know she'll end up on the street after fighting with the cab driver. She is very territorial and imperious, but what saves her is her great sense of humor. She would say that I remember only the bad things about my childhood and that I have a flair for distortion and melodrama. Which is probably true! I think the mother-daughter relationship is the primal relationship on the planet. Other things will come and go, but this relationship is forever. I still talk to my mother several times a week, and we have gone through our ups and downs.

JH: Did you inherit any of her qualities?

Well, one likes to think one has inherited the best of what one's mother has to offer. There is an essence of her in the Lourdes character in *Dreaming in Cuban*. For example, the way Lourdes defends Pilar and her painting even though she herself is appalled by it. That is what I respect most about my mother, that sense of loyalty. My mother is wonderful in a crisis actually more than in day-to-day things. She is definitely a strong, intelligent, funny person. I think the fact that I had to meet her standards growing up made working anywhere else a piece of cake.

JH: You have worked and lived in many cities in the United States. Where do you feel most at home?

Probably more than anything I subscribe to Salman Rushdie's idea of the homeland being on the page. That is where I feel most at home, in my head. I don't feel identified with California in the least, but it has been a good place for me to work. For me, identity is more emotional, intellectual, and fictional but not so much geographic at this point. And it is terrible because I am always trying to find the perfect place. Alastair Reid, the poet and translator, once told me that it doesn't really matter where you are because you live where you are working. I always try to remember that whenever I feel confined geographically. That it would be the same anywhere else.

(6)

Pa'lante

An Interview with Nicholasa Mohr

Nicholasa Mohr was born in 1935 in Manhattan's El Barrio of Puerto Rican parentage and raised in the Bronx, New York. Today she lives in the Park Slope section of Brooklyn. She has been writing successfully since 1973, and in many ways she is a precursor to the other women writers in this book.

We interviewed Mohr twice by telephone. In winter 1997 I was able to meet with her in her brownstone in Brooklyn to discuss the significance of being a Puerto Rican writer in the United States, her works, and the craft of writing. From the moment I walked into her home I found myself in a museum. There are artworks from all over the world—masks, drawings, etchings, calligraphy, and, most important, her own work done before she began to write. Her most impressive illustrations have to do with motherhood, the female body, and children. Not only is her home like a museum, but it's a spiritual haven. This is the home of someone who has struggled all her life and finally has peace. Her sons are grown, she lives alone, works alone in an office in her home. She likes being alone, having her own life, as she says, not having to answer to anyone.

Over Chinese herbal tea, we discussed life, books, spiritual awakenings, and other writers. What emerged was an extraordinarily complex writer who has experienced many cultures, and a humble writer in the sense that she al-

*ways feels grateful to be able to write for a living and to speak to so many
people through her works.*

   *Unlike many of the other women in this book, she has never had to teach
for a living, although she has been a visiting professor and a writer in residence. Mohr excels in the short story but also loves writing plays and screen-
plays. She has produced several novels and a memoir and, in our interview,
confessed that she is beginning to write poetry. Although for eight years no
new work was published, she was working and writing during that time.*

   Mohr's more well known works are Nilda *(1973),* El Bronx Remembered
(1975), In Nueva York *(1977),* Felita *(1979),* Rituals of Survival *(1985), and*
A Matter of Pride and Other Stories *(1997). She also published a memoir,*
Growing Up in the Sanctuary of My Imagination *(1994). She received the
Hispanic Heritage Award in 1997 and wrote the introduction for* Latinas:
Women of Achievement, *something she said she was honored to do. More
recently Mohr has been involved in theatre.* El Bronx Remembered *has
been successfully performed off Broadway and Mohr received a grant from the
New York State Council on the Arts to develop a musical drama based on
her novel* Nilda. *We began our discussion with what happened during her
years of silence. As she says, "Being a full-time writer is a tough commitment.
It doesn't matter what your race or gender is." She admits that, after many
years of production, she was "somewhat exhausted" by it all.*

                                                                    B.K.

BK: What happened between 1986 and 1994, the year your partial autobiography, *Growing Up in the Sanctuary of My Imagination,* was published?
There was a long period of silence from you in terms of published works.

I think I might have been somewhat exhausted. I had put out a number
of books before that. Being a full-time writer can be a tough commitment. It doesn't matter what your race or gender is, in our society it is
difficult to make a living in this field. And then being female from a
Latino group, being Puerto Rican, which even within the Hispanic or
Latino hierarchy is sometimes regarded as a people without a country
(although we are not without a nation, we have a nation), it's even more
difficult. The period 1986-1994 was a time of gestation. I needed to
gather myself together to begin again. Publishers had been asking me to
do work, and I started a couple of books after 1986 with some major

houses, but they weren't satisfied and I wasn't satisfied. So we just called it off.

I didn't want to do the memoir, but the publishers kept persisting. The memoir covers only up to the age of fourteen. I wanted to write a memoir that would explore the creative process and how that helped me endure, overcome, and succeed during those early years. Instead of chronological accounts, such as "I went to school with Mr. So and So," I wanted to explore just how my imagination really helped me survive and do more than survive. I wanted it to be exciting. My earliest memories intrigued me. Like when I was two and I figured out certain things. I wanted to recall growing up in the tenements, the barrio, growing up in the beginning of World War II. All this I found interesting.

BK: Your first visit to Puerto Rico is not described in the partial autobiography. What was it like?

It was a shock to me. My parents were from Puerto Rico. They remembered it as a paradise. But that was an illusion because it wasn't quite like that. You're called a "Yanqui" or a "Gringa." I went again on my honeymoon, when I was still quite young. I write about it in my collection of short stories, *A Matter of Pride*. Because I didn't grow up in Puerto Rico, I never knew Puerto Rico, so I don't have those childhood memories. I remember speaking at Fordham University a few years ago with other writers, a Jewish man from Australia, a wonderful female Indian poet, and a male poet from the Nuyorican poets' cradle, although he wasn't Latino. They had all been born in other countries, and when they spoke it was with such nostalgia, about the smells, sounds, and tender images. I felt so deprived! I was born in el barrio! I felt if I had been in Puerto Rico I too would have felt nostalgia and shared such experiences. But of course, I couldn't. Although I also love New York City and appreciate it as my hometown.

BK: In your memoir you describe the discovery of words and art as a magical and simultaneous moment. Can you describe this discovery in more detail?

Because there was nobody in the house to play with, all my older brothers were in school, I was extremely bored as a child. My mother was sick of my mischief and would dole out cocotazos every time I did something wrong. It was when I discovered drawing that I was finally at peace. I was finally seen as a good girl. For me, the magic was that I could take a blank piece of paper and immediately put a line dividing the paper from top to bottom and I would have two sections. All of the sudden I realized that I could do anything with a pencil. I could make this kind of magic and, as a little girl, that was mind-blowing.

The second discovery was that I could read what people were saying through words. There was no television at the time either. Of course, I might be illiterate today if there had been. [Laughs] We didn't have an enormous amount of books, we didn't have a library in our house, so I read labels on cans or what was written on cereal boxes, and even that was very stimulating. My great joy was the first time I went to the library. I was thrilled beyond anything to see all these books. I got my library card when I was seven. I taught myself to read and write. At the age of eleven I was picking up Agatha Christie and Jack London. Then I started reading *True Confessions* and love and romance magazines. Many of the mothers on my street would say, "Oh, eso es una cochinería." My mother replied, "I don't care what she reads, as long as she reads." I was through with the magazines by the time I was twelve. I was through with Frank Yerby and romance novels by the time I was thirteen, and by the time I was fourteen I was already into reading plays by Bernard Shaw and Eugene O'Neill and the fiction of Carson McCullers. So when I began to write in my early thirties for the first time it was all there, and even though I never studied writing, and never thought I would write professionally, I had prepared for it all of my life. I made the transition.

BK: How about the transition from artist to writer? Are you happy with your choice?

After twenty-five years, whether I'm happy or not is almost irrelevant. Here I am inundated with the world and the wonder of words! [Laughs] The writing came easy to me in the sense that I didn't have to worry about the skill. Perhaps that's because I had been trained as a visual artist. Any creative process has a life of its own in the sense that whether you are creating music or film, or in the plastic arts, there is a procedure that one must go through as a creative person. You must have a vision, an idea, and you have to make that work. You understand as a creative professional that you need all of the ingredients to get that product finished. As I was transferring all these skills that I had a learned as a visual artist—knowing when something works, knowing when your ideas are becoming concrete and crystallizing into something that others would be interested in—I was learning my craft as a writer. I see that when I read my earlier works today. I see that I would probably write them differently today. But that's O.K., because anything that one does is part of a development. I don't know if I would have been able to grasp the craft of writing as easily had I not had all that training as a visual artist. I don't know that if I had started out as a writer I would not have had to pay my dues as a creative worker in the ways that I had already done as a visual artist. But I do think I would have been a writer, a creative person, despite everything. It's karmic. I might have been a writer in another life. And I would have been creative even if I was born Caucasian, six feet tall, and with male genitals. I would just be a lot more arrogant! [Laughs] And who you are is so important as to the way and manner in which you create. I write what I write for no other reasons than who I am. We create out of what we know.

BK: Who are some of the writers who have influenced you and who you enjoy reading?

I was influenced by a lot of people. Shirley Jackson, a wonderful short story writer, Anton Chekhov, Carson McCullers, and Eudora Welty. I love the short story writers. My very favorite writers are a lot of female writers of the American South. There is something about the strength of some of those Southern writers. They are so powerful.

For reading, I have an eclectic sense. I like the new writers. I like a lot of the Chicana writers. I think they are all wonderful. I like the poetry of Pat Mora. I think she is great. I also like Alba Ambert and Esmeralda Santiago. I like Jack Agüeros, a good fiction writer and poet. I like Adrienne Rich. She's incredible. I like Helena María Viramontes. I like all of them. One annoying aspect about being a writer is that you don't read as much as you'd like. You are usually so busy writing that time is not so available.

I didn't read too many Latin American writers in Spanish when I was growing up because my Spanish was not up to it. I mean, I read the newspaper in Spanish, but to read books would have taken me a year with a dictionary. I read the translations of Jorge Luis Borges and Julio Cortázar. Both are challenging writers. You don't just melt into their work. And I still think García Márquez's *One Hundred Years of Solitude* is his best work. Later I was able to read a little Borges and García Marquéz in Spanish. But mostly I read anyone who has been translated into English, like Federico García Lorca and Pablo Neruda. I've been reading them since I was a kid. I always had a great sympathy for García Lorca's political views. And I also love the poetry of Julia de Burgos. I sought out her book. I had to go out and find it. It wasn't translated yet, so I had to read it in Spanish. I was determined to take a dictionary and sit down and read her work. That was in the late sixties.

JH: What do you like about Chicana writers? You mentioned Helena María Viramontes.

I like her complexity. I like that she goes through many shades to say something. She also is not easy. But she is interesting. Personally I like to write so that people melt into the work, but there is also this other kind of writing that I also appreciate, like Viramontes.

BK: Do you ever write in Spanish?

No. I can't write creatively in Spanish. I can write a letter in Puerto Rican Spanish, but I have to write in English. I don't have the formal education in Spanish and sadly am unable to do that.

JH: What inspires you to write?

The writing is an urge, it's not an inspiration. It's an urge. It's like you have to go to the bathroom, you have to write something creative. But what you write then is inspired by ideas and feelings. A need to put that down in an imaginative way, a need to express these feelings in a particular, very personal vocabulary that expresses itself through the medium of writing or painting or whatever. But of the craft itself, the writing, I'm never inspired to write! I mean, sometimes I don't want to write anything. I would rather wash floors. It can be very grueling. ¡Ay Dios! Do you think I want to sit down and write this book? I want to be out paseando all the time! [Laughs] Once you get the inspiration, you say, "Well, gosh, this idea is eating away at me," and you go with it! Then you have to write. I would say that it is probably the same for anybody that's doing creative work. And of course, I'm in a situation where I better work or Con Edison is going to turn off my lights or I will be dispossessed! [Laughs] And that's another kind of inspiration!

JH: What about your mother? How was she an influence on you as a writer?

My mother loved to tell stories. Although she had no formal education, she had a marvelous way of speaking. She was very smart, very bright. At one time the Puerto Rican community loved to tell stories. I don't know if that still goes on in Puerto Rico today. But at one time we would get together and tell stories. Like other communities and people who come from rural areas, their form of literature is an oral tradition. That was exciting because people would even invent stories. My mother would tell me the famous Juan Bobo stories, about this simple trickster. When things were bad, or we didn't have enough to eat and there was a lot of stress, someone would always tell us a story. That kind of storytelling was encouraged by my mother because she had to entertain all those children and she often did it by telling stories. She had a free and wonderful imagination.

JH: How do you look back on your three early works *Nilda*, *El Bronx Remembered*, and *In Nueva York*? What have you learned from them?

There are a couple of things I have learned. The first thing is that I realize how much I love to tell stories. I also learned that I liked the idea that my books could be part of popular culture in a way that my art could not be. As a writer, what I realized almost overnight was that anyone could read my books. Anyone could go to the library and read my books for nothing. In paperback people can buy them for relatively cheap prices. That made me happy. I also didn't have to deal with middle-class collectors, bourgeois collectors, who give me a pain in my petunia. They can be awful. For example, they buy a print or a drawing and want to know what you had for lunch the day before, what kind of sheets you use on your bed, and if you have any hobbies! It was a relief to be free of that. But real satisfaction came in the fact that anyone could read my work. And I look back at my earlier work and see that it's much more visual than my later work, probably because I was still thinking primarily as a visual artist.

Finally, as I was writing *Felita* I realized that *Nilda, El Bronx Remembered,* and *In Nueva York* follow a chronological order. They go from World War II to the time I was hanging around in the streets of El Bronx as a kid in the late forties and fifties, up to the Vietnam War. Suddenly I realized that I had unconsciously done three books on my personal history because there was nothing about Latinos here and certainly nothing about Puerto Ricans. It wasn't until my fourth book that I could write about contemporary times. It is as if I had to validate my existence as a Latina in the United States, my personal history. That was for me a true revelation.

BK: Throughout your career you've worked in every genre except poetry. Did you ever write poetry?

I'm thinking of writing poetry now. I'm doing a few poems now because I have to be stimulated. I admire poets so much. I think they are so fabulous because they can spend two days on a sentence. I might have a whole story out by then! [Laughs] One has to have mucha paciencia and be truly inspired to bring out the right metaphor. At one point I thought I would never write a poem, but now I'm beginning to think that it might be fun.

BK: Why now?

Because I think I've been through so many varied experiences in my life and feel that perhaps I can reflect about them in yet another sense. However, who knows, since I'm not altogether sure about going in this direction.

BK: What are the differences for you between the genres?

I don't think one is easier than the other. But my favorite form is the short story. For me, they take years to write. These stories are all like precious jewels to me. I put them in a drawer, then I take them out, and so on and so on. It's part of my oral history background, the cuentos. In a short story you have to be razor sharp, very frugal. For me, a kind of intense magic has to happen. With the novel you take your time, you can build, you can indulge yourself a little bit, you can relax in terms of having time to develop and embellish. The novel is a different challenge. It's similar to the difference of working as a printmaker doing a series of etchings and creating one painting. It's two distinct ways of approaching the creative process as a means to a goal. The same thing happens when you write for children or adults—the approach is somewhat different.

BK: Although *Nilda* is for young adults, I still enjoy it.

Well, actually, I didn't consciously write that for young adults. It was marketed that way. Nor did I write *El Bronx Remembered* or *In Nueva York* for young adults. Those three books were never targeted by me for young adults specifically. However, when I wrote *Felita* I made a conscious attempt to write for children. That was when I began to understand the difference between adult and children's fiction.

BK: What is the difference?

In a sense children don't understand irony. Or at least they don't understand irony in the way that adults do. Children are very innocent, and open. There's a certain unabashed truth that you must have for children. It's not easy communicating strongly that way, because although you can get a child's attention, to get a child involved in a meaningful way the writer must be totally honest. Kids will ask you anything and everything They're not interested in being polite and don't even know or care if they are hurting your feelings! [Laughs] So in writing for them you have to deal with human beings who are first developing and becoming conscious of the world. You must respect this and be part of their joyfulness and frustration as they struggle to comprehend and understand. Adults are already formed. I couldn't begin to write certain stories for kids that I would write for adults, and vice versa.

BK: You, along with Judith Ortiz Cofer and Sandra Cisneros, are very conscious of not neglecting children, younger adults.

Yes! When I was writing *Old Letivia and the Mountain of Sorrow*, a fairy tale, I was very involved in the fact that I wanted to write this tale for children, although I want everyone to enjoy my children's books. I also feel adults can enjoy them too, teachers and parents. But these books are for young people first and foremost; they are the ones that matter most in this instance.

BK: In some ways you're filling that blank space where you didn't see yourself represented in the literature.

That's right. Like in the *Song of el Coquí.* I have the character of the Guinea Hen who is perceived by the populace as ugly, which is a metaphor for the racism we have in Puerto Rico. But the Guinea is taken in by the mask maker who gives her a sense of pride, a pride or self-esteem that I want children to have. There's very little of that on the island.

JH: What's happening with the Nuyorican poets' café scene today?

It's very different. It's a showcase for poets from all over the United States and all over the world. It used to be a little storefront and there were mostly Nuyorican poets, like Sandra María Esteves, Pedro Pietri, and many others. It was Miguel Algarín's creation, who I believe is still influential in running it. It was his idea.

BK: How would you historically define that scene?

Well, I think that what happened was similar to the Yiddish theater in New York at the turn of the twentieth century. Historically, Yiddish theater was very influential in New York. It turned out a wealth of writers, comedians. I think that the Nuyorican period was a magical period when Latino poets and writers in New York began to be heard. That was also part of the Young Lords and the Black Panthers, part of the sensibility of the time. I believe that art and artists really define and give things a name. Artists define civilization for all of us and who we all are as a society. And I think that became true as a result of the Nuyorican scene. New York is a special place because people who come here own it. By being here in New York and contributing, this becomes your city. The tremendous influx of Jews made the Yiddish theater so incredible. Although Puerto Ricans have been in New York since the last century, we came in significant numbers first because of the tobacco workers, then after World War II, and later during the Vietnam War. I think it was a time when Miguel Algarín, and I don't know what motivated him, I would have to speak to him, put out a platform for Latino writing to be heard. And a lot of talented people came out of there. I did not, because I'm not a poet. At the time I was a visual artist. But I knew the group and I would go there. In the Museo del Barrio there was a taller, a workshop, that had many artists, so it was a time when we had a platform to define who we were culturally. It was exciting and we were all working like crazy.

JH: Do you see yourself writing more essays on historical moments like the Nuyorican scene?

Maybe. That's hard to say. Right now I am writing a children's book for Viking. After that, there's an off-Broadway group that would like to do a musical on *Nilda,* so I will be doing the book. I really don't know, qué sé yo!

BK: Has the relationship that you describe between the island and mainland Puerto Ricans in your essay "A Separation Beyond Language" changed at all?

I think it's changing, but I don't think it has totally changed. It still goes beyond language. Last year when I went to Puerto Rico I was at a taller in the Ateneo [a cultural center on the island], when we brought up racism. The response was, what racism? People were not going to own up to the racism and the classism in Puerto Rico. I may have to bring that essay up to date.

BK: What work are you most proud of?

That's very hard to say because you feel like you're talking about your children, you really love them all for different reasons. They're all different, and they all have a special quality. *The Magic Shell* is probably one the gentlest books I've written, and I can't say that I like it better or less than any other book. I think that *A Matter of Pride* is one of the toughest books I've ever written. The stories in *A Matter of Pride* are really tougher than those in *Rituals of Survival.* The women in *A Matter of Pride* are brutally honest. I think *A Matter of Pride* was a big despojo for me.

Everybody said, "Boy, you got even with everyone." I had a lot of things to say. I was relentless in that book. You know, when that book came out and I said to myself, My goodness, Nicholasa, WOW! What happened here! No mercy . . . Yes! [Laughs] But once a book is done, it's like giving birth and it's what it is. For me, it's creating a body of work in my lifetime, and this includes my visual art as well. As a creative person, I've always been very fortunate to make my living with my writing and my visual art. Even though I've had to hustle! And I had to take a lot of insults, but that is O.K. [Laughs] I'm not arrogant. I'm really grateful.

BK: What do you think about this generation of Latina writers coming out now and being recognized?

I think it's wonderful. I'm so happy. Alba Ambert and Esmeralda Santiago did a little thing at Boricua College here in Brooklyn and I was able to say some welcoming words. I met Julia Alvarez at Middlebury College when I was there as a keynote speaker. I like Dolores Prida, the playwright, Cubana raised in New York. I hope Piri Thomas will be doing another book. It's wonderful to have our own culture out there. I just read Alba Ambert's new book, *The Eighth Continent*. Whenever a Latina writer is published it just makes everyone else's work stronger. There is plenty of room, plenty of room for more, the more the better. We're all going to write in our own special way. No one is going to write the same story in the same way. I really feel great when I see writers coming out and being recognized. I think it's just fabulous! I just hope it doesn't disappear, because we've had this before. You know, sometimes we're popular for a whole seven minutes.

BK: In many respects you paved the way for them.

Well, in a way I guess I did, although I never thought about it too much. People used to say, "Aren't there any Puerto Rican writers?" But Puerto Rican writers were not being published. Except for Arte Público Press. They started publishing us when there were very few Latino writers on the larger literary scene. I just feel so happy that there is a whole library full of our books now and not just a shelf. So yes, I was there.

BK: What kind of criticism of your work would you like to see?

So much criticism takes a sociological tone that it feels like critics just don't feel what you are writing. Someone will ask me, "What do you think about the Puerto Ricans who had a march in Ohio?" and perhaps that week I won't even have read anything about it. Many interviews have so little to do with my writing and so much to do with the social-political circumstance. The Puerto Rican Diaspora keeps our literature in a subcategory. I'm put on a specialty shelf. I'm not seen. We are not seen, as a main staple or a main course. We're just the appetizer that you may or may not enjoy. Give us, as artists, the recognition as artists and writers, and do not confuse us with sociologists and political scientists. I have great respect for social scientists; let them answer these questions. Even the contemporary writers are criticized differently than Latino writers. I would like to see criticism like that done on Eudora Welty's work, where critics discuss the style, content, and impact that one's writing has on the greater society at large, globally.

BK: How did you balance having children and work, and what have your children taught you?

It certainly changed me as a woman. It just makes your sense of time different. I had two boys, David and Jason. That was very difficult to handle. My husband died, and I had these two boys to raise. Nonetheless, with children you just get through it, you never get it down, there's no set formula, you just get through. But I never wanted to say to my sons I could have been this or that but because of you. So I did it with veinte mil marronas. And that's how we all do it. My second son, Jason, presented me with another very big challenge in life. It was very difficult, but it became a time of learning. He is my best teacher in life, my son Jason. He has taught me what unconditional love really means, and about humility and understanding in a way that is beyond measure. One day I might write about it. Although these things have to come naturally, they have to find a way into one's writing so that it's never forced but instead becomes a welcome source of inspiration.

JH: How do you feel about having received the Hispanic Award?

Oh, I was very proud, very surprised and happy. It was a lovely surprise, and I was muy orgullosa because I really didn't expect to get it. After I was nominated I left for London. When I returned I got the notice. I'm extremely proud. I'm very happy when I get any award! [Laughs] I'm asking people to read my books, and I'm just happy when they do and they like my work. I'm not pompous about it at all, because there are a lot of talented people out there and if I'm chosen, hey, I thank the spirits, the gods, and . . . pa'lante!

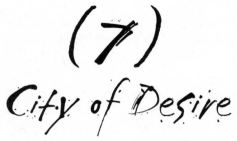

(7)
City of Desire

An Interview with Cherríe Moraga

Cherríe Moraga was born in Los Angeles, California, in 1952. She has lived in Boston and New York, and currently makes her home in San Francisco. Throughout her life she has been a social and political activist as well as a teacher and writer. She currently teaches in the Departments of Drama and Spanish at Stanford University and is a writer in residence at the Brava Theater Center, a multicultural women's organization in San Francisco, California.

For the past three decades, Moraga has been an active contributor to Latina cultural and literary production. This Bridge Called My Back: Radical Writings by Women of Color *(1981), coedited with Gloria Anzaldúa, and* Cuentos: Stories by Latinas *(1983), coedited with Alma Gómez and Mariana Romo-Carmona, are groundbreaking anthologies of Latina literature. In her autobiography,* Loving in the War Years *(1983), Moraga affirms her Chicana lesbianism through prose and poetry. In the play* Giving Up the Ghost *(1986), Moraga presents a philosophy that prevails throughout her works: she is "making familia from scratch," redefining the traditional concept of Family to an extended community. Her plays* Shadow of a Man *(1990),* Heroes and Saints *(1992), and* Watsonville *(1996) have received awards from the National Endowment for the Arts and the Fund for New American Plays.*

In the collection of essays and poems The Last Generation *(1993), Moraga is concerned with remembering the past, especially indigenous roots and land, to understand the present. She calls attention to the social transformations that are affecting indigenous communities, gays and lesbians of color, and youth. More than anything, Moraga reflects on what it means to lose one's culture through genocide and language.* The play Mexican Medea: The Hungry Woman, *a work in progress, focuses on a woman's loss of her child in a surreal, futuristic urban space. In her memoir,* Waiting in the Wings: A Portrait of a Queer Motherhood *(1997), Moraga explores the survival of the child of a Chicana lesbian in the face of death.*

We first spoke with Moraga at the conference "Hispanics: Cultural Locations" at the University of San Francisco in October 1997. We began the interview before she was to premier a reading from Waiting in the Wings, *a reading that turned out to be both inspiring and heart wrenching.*

I had the opportunity to meet with Moraga again one foggy morning in the spring of 1998 at Café Commons in the heart of the Mission in San Francisco, California. We talked about writers such as Federico García Lorca and Leslie Marmon Silko whose works are dedicated to tracing their indigenous roots and writers such as James Baldwin and Junot Díaz whose works engage the theme of desire. Down-to-earth, witty, and profound, Moraga spoke of the connection between writing and teaching and the importance of bridging the worlds of academia and the Chicano/Latino community. Teaching and cultivating a new generation of writers have enriched her life because this younger generation has become an extension of her family, a community, that will contribute to the growing body of Chicano/Latino arts and letters. She says of her students, "I love it when someone falls in love with being an artist and starts to learn the skills about how to make a life that way!" Desire and passion are the elements that she hopes to pass on to the next generation. As a writer, Moraga has come a long way, from her radical days as a social activist writer at Kitchen Table Press to her role as a queer Chicana mother writer to her angelic son, Rafa.

J.H.

JH: When did you realize that you wanted to write?

When I was very young, I drew and played music. It was a long journey before I actually got to the word because really I was a very poor reader. My relationship was to the spoken story, and I think that is why I write plays. It was very much oral. My mother and her family, her generation, all my tías, were wonderful storytellers! But my mother was the best. She is a premier storyteller! My sister was an incredible reader, and she would tell me what the stories were about. As a young person, literature came through my sister's mouth and stories came through my mother's mouth. When I was in high school I wrote and received a lot of affirmation from writing. I got a scholarship to go to a private college in Los Angeles. My sister, my brother, and I were the first to go to college, so there was no precedent for me to know how one maneuvers that world. When I sat in a class on Chaucer and Beowulf, I remember that the professor wrote from one end of the board to the other. It was one of those blackboards on three walls, and I had no idea what the man was talking about. I decided at that point that I was going to read every single book I could get my hands on. That was very pivotal to my writing, because what happened is that by beginning to read I fell in love with literature and with what one could know about human meaning through literature. It was always exciting to me how through writing and literary analysis you could talk about human concerns.

JH: Do you remember which writers had an impact on you?

There have been pivotal moments in which something that I read affected a change in my writing or gave me the conviction to continue to write. I was reading a long, long poem by Judy Grahn called "A Woman Is Talking to Death." It's a poem by a white working-class lesbian poet who was really influential in the early 1970s in the lesbian literature movement. I encountered her work through these workshops and writers in the Bay Area in 1977. I was so impressed by this piece of work because the writing was about poverty. She was writing not just about economic poverty, the way one looks at class, but also about the poverty of being nobody, being considered a nobody by the world. The poem is the woman's encounter with death, both physically and spiritually. And it just blew me out of the water because it showed me that there was a way to write about identity and poverty, and by association race, that was beautiful literature and very heart wrenching. Different writers have affected me in different ways. When I discovered the works of James Baldwin, I was so moved because he could write with such honesty about desire, not only homosexual desire but heterosexual desire. He understood the function of desire and its relationship to spirit and also to political change. That, to me, is revolutionary. Now, in the last five years, the works of Leslie Marmon Silko have had a great impact on me. I feel that there are connections that she is making in terms of a kind of writing that we have to do to counter the death dealings of a Euro-American monoculture. She is also a wonderful storyteller, so I find courage in that kind of writing and being able to have that kind of worldview that is based on her own indigenism. I feel that we Chicanas could be drawing from that source much more than we are. I find her very inspiring.

JH: You've discussed the need to return to a language. What do you mean by that?

It involves privilege of being the first-generation writer, being a writer who gets education, who is coming from a working-class background. Dorothy Allison is a good example of that as she is also from a working-class background. Her writing uses a curious mix of first-generation education and roots, which in her case are oral. As a writer, I feel that my language continues to evolve because it means access to craft in the sense of really trying to learn how to control the language: to describe and to reflect best your own sensibility. It also requires further digging into your colloquial voice, the voice of culture and its nuances. Theater allowed me to hear and make literature out of the wealth of voices from my culture. But I never write the way people talk! I try to make poetry out of those combinations. Even though I listened to my mother talk, it was very visual. Her descriptions were like watching a movie. She could talk about the crease in a man's pants, the shape of light coming into the room, all of which had emotion. She remembers in images, and so the images have emotional meaning. I learned that from my mama. That is what I mean about a return to an original language. You can do it in Spanish, English, street colloquialisms, all the languages that as an urban person I inhabit.

JH: What do you enjoy about teaching at Stanford and at Brava? How are these experiences similar or different?

At Stanford I was hired to teach creative writing, Latino theater, or new courses like "Radical Latina Scholarship." The majority of my students are women of color. So this is an incredible opportunity for me. But not for a minute do I forget that this is Stanford University, definitely the belly of the beast! Sometimes I feel that the academy makes you stupid. It makes students produce at a rate that does not allow for real thoughtful questions. If I get the opportunity to work a number of years with certain students, then we can slow the process down. If I can work with young writers of color for four consecutive years and give them the opportunity to see one way to do art, maybe when they leave, they can take that knowledge with them. I find that so exciting. I love it when someone falls in love with being an artist and starts to learn the skills about how to make a life that way.

Working with Brava was wonderful for me. (Moraga had a residency with Brava from 1990 to 1996.) To teach outside the university is the best. The difficulty is trying to make a living at the same time. When I was teaching "Drama Divas" [a theater troupe composed primarily of queer youth of color], they wrote about their lives. They acted based on their lives, and they played each other's lives. That had a direct relationship to their empowerment when they walked into the streets. There was no disconnection. The art affected their daily lives. It changed them. It changed their consciousness on a living basis. They acted on what they thought. You never see such direct results in the university setting. Another course I taught for Brava was "Indigena as Scribe." The group contained Chicana, Latina, and Native women from different backgrounds, anywhere from twenty-five to sixty-five years old,: most of them working outside the university. We met about once a week for four years. I kept working with the same group of people until we were done. There was a sense that those three hours a week were very sagrado. If you live up to your writing, your life changes. It was not therapy. It was always focused on the writing. You never say to writers, "I'm sorry this happened to you." That is never the goal. You ask the writer, How can you make the best art from your pain?

BK: How do you balance writing and teaching?

Well, I love teaching. I think that there are only a certain number of things that you can do in this life. I spent a number of years doing political organizing as well as teaching and writing. I think one of the decisions that I finally made was that I couldn't do it all. The order of my priorities had to change, and my writing had to come first, no matter what! When I decided in my twenties that I was going to be a writer, I made a decision to evaluate the "success" of each year based on whether or not I got more time to write. I would wait tables, clean houses, paint offices. I did all these nontraditional jobs so that I could avoid a nine-to-five job and have more time to write. In terms of teaching young students, the amount of talent out there is awesome, but this by itself means nothing. What makes a writer is discipline. Sometimes I feel like I haven't even begun to write the way that I want to in my life. My major interest is to develop that discipline: working with kids of color, particularly Chicanos and specifically Chicanas. From my creative writing and theater classes in the past, many students have gone on to film school and received M.F.A.s all over the country and there are others that are beginning to be published. So I guess, in many ways, my goals as a teacher are being realized.

I am very fortunate in recent years in that there is a kind of balance in my life between my work as a writer and my "work" to make a living. I know my art comes first, and I have less and less problems saying no to people regarding other demands on my time (for my son)! What I lament, of course, in a university system, especially ethnic studies programs, is that there is a generation of critics being developed but not its creators. The departments are doing little to cultivate a new generation of creative artists.

BK: What is your rapport with critics and literary criticism?

If a critical writer can point out an absence in the work, because they value the work so that they want more from it, more power to them and to me. I appreciate that. That, to me, is one of the best examples of criticism that I find is useful to me as a writer, one that requires more from me, one that really "reads" not only what I say but also what I long to say. I don't read a lot of criticism, not because it may hurt my feelings, not because it is negative, but because it is reductionist, where a critic enters the work full of his own prejudices. It makes me feel cheap, something you thought was grand . . .

JH: Have you read Yvonne Yarbro-Bejarano's criticism of your works?

Yes, I mean we are colleagues now at Stanford. We met by phone in 1985 when she was working on a critical essay on *Giving Up the Ghost*. We are in dialogue about my work and the work of other Chicana writers because we know each other as friends. I mean, how many Chicana lesbian critics are out there with her reputation, insights, and ability? So I really value her and learn a great deal from her. But we don't always agree. I'll ask, Why are you worrying about that? That's not a concern of mine. That is on a friend level. As a critic, she will go ahead and do what she needs to do. That is totally her prerogative whether I like it or not. It is a good relationship. It is how academic Chicana critics face how you deal with living writers. We need her. She has done a lot of work with popular culture and performance as well as literature.

JH: Do you see a dialogue happening between Mexican and Chicana writers in the near future? If so, along what lines?

Well, I think it's very problematic because of the race and class differences, but there have been some openings. Elena Poniatowska wrote a pivotal article about Chicana writers. She thought that Mexican women writers had a great deal to learn from Chicana writers. If I remember correctly, we had the courage to write about things that their class privilege did not allow them. We were writing about identity, sexuality, and race in ways that they could not conceive of doing. So they should be reading us. And I thought that was a pretty great thing. I remember writing her a letter to thank her, and she wrote me a very beautiful letter back. I think that is very important. I have been reading more Mexican literature lately, Elena Garro, Rosario Castellanos, and others.

JH: Is reading in Spanish a different experience?

Oh, yeah! But if I read in English, I can do it faster for my fiction class at Stanford. I was teaching *Balún Canán* by Rosario Castellanos. I had read it originally in Spanish, but then the time crunch came down and I had to reread it, so I read it more quickly in English to refresh my memory. The book was a completely different experience for me! It was so shallow for me in English. In Spanish it had so much resonance for me because she is experimenting with language in a way that the English translation does not capture.

JH: She is also a poet, so you miss out on other linguistic experimentations as well.

Right. I had a conversation with Hélène Cixous, the French writer and critic, who is also a playwright and has written a number of articles about writing that I find very inspiring. She also speaks at least four different languages. She was talking about the problems of people translating her work and the problems of translation. It finally made sense to me. When a writer is writing in her original language, the accidents that happen in language are all coming out of his unconscious. So what you are experiencing in the original language is the unconscious, not just the story. When you translate, you have to lose that. You can't re-create in another language the unconscious of a writer because that only happens in the miracle of how she puts together the exact words at that moment. It was an incredible thought to me.

BK: Do you find Spanglish problematic or impure, that it poses a danger to Hispanic culture?

That is a colonial and classist mentality. It is ridiculous! It is the whole purity question of "proper Spanish," castellano. I remember in 1985 sitting in the Intar Theatre in New York among Puerto Rican, Cuban, and Colombian playwrights and I was the only Chicana, the only one writing in two languages in the context of that New York theater world. I was the only one doing it, and now everyone is doing it. Everyone thought it was so new. But I thought, Chicano theater has been doing this since 1968, THANK YOU VERY MUCH! My formal training is not in Spanish, so largely my Spanglish comes out when I am doing characters because they would speak that way. I appreciate having access to two languages to manipulate the voice, the characterization, the poetry of speakers. English has a very different rhythm, so when you choose to use that rhythm versus the softer, lyrical rhythm of Spanish, it is a totally calculated decision. My first versions are not calculated, but when I finally finish a work, it is all about fine tuning. It is so wonderful to give a poetic voice to this combination. As U.S. Latinos, it's interesting to observe when the Spanish comes out, when the English comes out. What do you speak when you are making love? What do you speak when you are pissed off at your kid?

JH: Speaking of poetic voice, how has the craft of poetry enhanced the writing of other genres?

Lorna Dee Cervantes is our Chicano poet laureate. I have an enormous amount of respect for her as a poet. I feel that poetry is her genre. I can't say the same for myself. But what I realized is that, for me, starting as a poet is the best place to start writing in any genre. The poet is always about the condensed moment. Poetry is the studied economical use of language, which all genres should require. It is the syntax of the moment, not just the syntax of the palabra. It's about how you put two moments next to each other to illuminate a small truth. If you write plays in that manner, it can still sound colloquial, which has always been my goal. How do you make poetry sound colloquial? The poet's sensibility creates the richest writers, fiction or nonfiction. Many people in theater feel that language is not important, that action is what counts. I'm not that kind of writer. I always feel that I'm a poet, and that sensibility enters every genre I work in.

JH: Could you discuss the process of creating *Waiting in the Wings*? It's a critical moment in your life.

I never intended to write *Wings*. I always keep journals religiously. So I had journal entries dating from my son's conception—I think because of the process of being pregnant, spending so much time being alone. With so much physical change going on, my journal entries deepened. I was filled with a dream life. When my son was born premature and became ill, I felt I was just an animal. I thought only of my child's survival. There was nothing, no one else. Nearly a year later, when he had completely gained his health, I began to type up these journal entries. I needed to feel again that I was a creative person. Creating a child is not the same as creating art. I think they get collapsed and that is not true. I hungered for something else beyond survival. I wanted art again in my life.

JH: How do you make a distinction between those two kinds of creativity?

As I typed up these journal entries, I discovered that I had about one hundred pages. When I read them, I realized that there was a story there. The story had to do with la enfrentación con la muerte. The most intimate being is the one that comes out of you, and in my case that being was to embody my confrontation with death. It changed everything. That is why I called Rafa my teacher at the time. I felt like his choice to stay on the planet and the way he came in to it had history and meaning. That affected my spirit and sense of the continuity of our existence. If he could decide to come for two weeks and leave, that was his choice. I could not do anything about that. That little being changed my viewpoint in such a fundamental way. That is what I wanted to write about. The book ends with the death of my uncle, who is very dear to me. I realize that my family is dying. My mother is in her eighties. It's like living with the daily knowledge of death. So the book ends up being that kind of meditation. I thoroughly loved writing that book because it gave me the opportunity to contemplar those questions.

JH: As a mother, has that experience changed your attitude toward writing?

It has only made me more vigilant to get the work done, since caring for a small child requires so much time, not only in terms of hours, but emotional time as well. I sleep less and have learned to write at night.

JH: What motivated you to rework Greek mythology in your play, *Mexican Medea: The Hungry Woman*?

For many years I was interested in La Llorona (the weeping woman) and her connection to Malinche. I had read Rudolfo Anaya's version of the story. I got really upset. I'm so tired of hearing how this woman killed her children because a man dumped her. Similarly, when I read Octavio Paz's work [*Labyrinths of Solitude*] on Malinche, it made me angry. But those are great gifts! I thank Rudy. I thank Paz. Their texts gave me the stimulus to respond. Sometimes it takes you many years to figure out what the respuesta is. When I read Euripedes's *Medea*, I immediately recognized her as a Mexican woman. I also saw Passolini's film version of *Medea*. He depicts Medea by having Maria Callas portray her. I saw this dark Greek woman and it had such an impact on me. She is considered a very uncouth sorceress. I thought, she is just too much mujer for the world. These are issues that I want to talk about. What people fear about Medea and La Llorona is their power to give birth and to take life away, like the Aztec goddess Coatlicue. It is that side of woman that is the opposite of La Vírgen of Guadalupe, that passivity. It is that pasión, that coraje, that venganza that man or the culture of men fear! That is what I was interested in exploring.

JH: It seems as if the hunger goes beyond the physical aspects of her body and is more related to her mind.

In the process of writing my Chicana version, I ran into the myth of the "Hungry Woman" in Aztec culture. It's a creation myth about a woman with holes in her body. It's interesting because that is what Don Juan talks about in Carlos Castañeda's book. He says that when a woman has a child, it leaves a hole in her body. I've written about that aspect in some of my plays like *Heroes and Saints*. In the myth they say that the spirits came down and tried to fill the holes in her body by creating in their places rivers, mountains, and more. She could never be satisfied and was always heard moaning and crying. I think it's fascinating because the myth describes the primordial state of female hunger. And the hunger is prememory. The Llorona is not looking for her lost children but herself. She is looking for her lost womanhood. These are all patriarchal myths. If you feel that as a woman, as a Chicana, that you have been born hungry, that fuerza, the power of what you could be, comes to you. By returning to that primordial state, I wanted to know what happens to a Chicana when she recognizes that memory of being something bigger than this racist world. My thoughts are that a woman kills her children when they are no longer her own. It's an act of suicide rather than homocide in the sense that she is killing part of herself. This has been the most challenging work for me to write for all the reasons I just mentioned.

JH: How do you find a sense of community with other writers?

I think it is a measure of our age, of our so-called professional status as writers, that we don't get involved with each other much in the process. We just see the published works of other Chicana writers, of African-American writers, and that becomes part of our own dialogue with ourselves. When we were younger there was much more dialogue among Chicana writers because we were all coming up and we needed support. But now, you are just really busy with your career and your life, and I lament that. The best conference I ever attended in my life featured Dorothy Allison, Leslie Marmon Silko, Grace Payley, myself, Paule Marshall, Toni Cade Bambara, and others. It was organized by Diana Taylor at Dartmouth. The incredible thing was that there was not one critic. It was a dialogue among creative writers. Do you know how rare it is to talk to peers about your work? Everyone was taking notes, people were listening, and not one critic was interpreting us. And that is the thing we should be doing among Chicanas! I have a lot of questions for Sandra, for Ana, for Denise, for Gloria, for Helena, for everyone! I would also like to include visual artists in the dialogue.

JH: How do you feel about México? Do you travel there often?

I've done extensive travel in México, but I don't have family there. I love México, although my trips are always uncomfortable. They always agitate me, because you are part and you are not part of it. When you see the colonial relationship between the United States and México, you can't have consciousness and have a good time! It is always a very disturbing yet rich experience. The land, that is the best! That is the reason I like to go there, especially the southern part. I've visited the pyramids, the ruinas. I have also studied a lot of Mesoamerican, pre-Columbian history. It is always very relaxing for me, and it also affects my work as you have seen. I always feel that when I go down to México, I go as a student.

BK: What kind of home is for you there, and what kind of home is for you here?

There is no home for me in México, except the land. The deserts. I spent time in Sonora and Chihuahua a couple of summers ago. It's the land. These are my raíces. My family is from Sonora. The land calms me down, opens me up. I feel like it is a very rich resource in my writing. I experience a quietness there that is difficult to conjure in this country.

JH: Would you ever reside in Mexico?

I hope to do that for periods of time. Particularly when you have a kid, your priorities change. I feel like I want to give my kid what I did not get: a direct sense of Mexican culture and some spots of land without Gringo interference. He can decide what he wants to do with it. I would really love for him not have to struggle with language the way I have had to, and on some level, since we have no relatives in México, for him to know that all of this North and South is his ancestral land.

(8)
The Poetic Truth

An Interview with Judith Ortiz Cofer

Judith Ortiz Cofer was born in Hormigueros, Puerto Rico, in 1952 and moved to the United States with her family in 1955. Although her family made their permanent home in Paterson, New Jersey, she frequently traveled back and forth between New Jersey and Puerto Rico, an experience she describes in detail in her "partial" autobiography, Silent Dancing. *Our interview with Cofer immediately took off with a discussion on the craft of writing. She described in great detail the process of writing, spoke at length on the difference between the novel and poetry with striking images, and told of how she confronted the women in her family to develop her own poetic truth. For Ortiz Cofer, poetry is like deep analysis because it allows her to wander into places where she normally would not go. The difference between poetry and the novel is like that between brain surgery and any other surgery: "Both are difficult, but one requires the skill of a diamond cutter." And she is especially ardent about debunking the myth of inspiration. Inspiration is not a "thunderbolt" but rather a culmination of daily obsessions that evolve from "notes on cards" that she stuffs in her purse to create the final work.*

Ortiz Cofer, along with Nicholasa Mohr, has the distinction of being one of the first and still few Puerto Rican woman writers to write in English. Her work is distinct from other Puerto Rican writers in the sense that she lives and writes outside of New York City. She does not consider herself a

Nuyorican writer, because she did not grow up in New York and because she does not use language in the same way. She tells of a time when Nicolás Kanellos introduced her by saying, "There are the Nuyorican writers and there are the island writers and there is Judith Ortiz Cofer."

Cofer received her M. A. in creative writing from Florida Atlantic University. Currently she is a professor of English and creative writing at the University of Georgia in Athens. Her poems, short stories, and essays have been published since 1977 in many magazines, including the Americas Review, Kenyon Review, *and the* Georgia Review. *Her works include* The Year of Our Revolution *(1998);* An Island Like You: Stories of the Barrio *(1995), a collection of short stories for young adults; two collections of poetry published in 1987,* Reaching for the Mainland *and* Terms of Survival; *and a collection of prose and poetry,* The Latin Deli *(1993). Her memoir,* Silent Dancing: A Partial Remembrance of a Puerto Rican Childhood, *and novel,* The Line of the Sun, *were both published in 1990 and have been translated into Spanish. Her novel was nominated for a National Book Award. We began our discussion with her pragmatic approach to writing and the muse, which, she jokes, is female and only visits male writers in Hollywood.*

B.K.

BK: You once said that you don't believe in the muse. Why?

Although my writing gives me a spiritual life, I don't depend on anything extraordinary or supernatural or this thing called inspiration, which I believe is something other than what most people think it is. In my essay "5:00 A.M." in *The Latin Deli,* I said that for me the mysterious part is why I need to write. I need to write like some people need to run, like some people need to play a musical instrument, or like some people need to cook as a form of self-expression. Actually, I don't write for self-expression but for self-discovery. I started giving myself an assigned time, which was five to seven in the morning before my child got up and I had to prepare for my job and everything else. I found that I could will myself to be creative at that hour and that it was a process very similar to exercise. I don't like to exercise, but at a certain point in my day I say that I'm going to do an hour of exercise because I need to. If I don't, I'll regret it and my day will be less than it should be. So I found that it's a combination of the mystical and the practical.

I've always known that if I don't carve a little time for myself, then I won't write. And it's not inspiration. I always tell my students that if the muse does exist she's female and only goes to writers on the West Coast, male writers on the West Coast, who can make her famous in Hollywood. But seriously, I believe that inspiration is actually the culmination of a process of gestation. I believe that I start thinking about something I want to do and it obsesses me. I take notes on cards and put them in my purse, and at a certain point I need to sit down and work on it. For me, that's the point that most people call inspiration. But it's not a thunderbolt. It's been happening. You've been programming your brain, you've been getting ready for that moment. It's more of a natural than a supernatural process.

BK: Is writing a process you enjoy?

Who said I enjoyed writing?! [Laughs] I think that writing is one of the hardest, most painful of human endeavors. When I said that I experienced a moment of joy, the pain I have to go through for that moment of joy is only sometimes worth it. Because sometimes you go through the pain and the moment of joy doesn't come. What I'm saying is that I'm like that runner who is addicted to the high on reaching that third mile. Before then, of course, every bone hurts, every muscle hurts, and then there's that moment when those endorphins are released. But it's always a fearsome proposition to begin something new, and so the answer is no, I don't always enjoy writing. Some days I wish I could put my energies and intelligence into real estate! I'd be rich if I put into examining the stock market all the effort I put into writing a poem.

BK: But there must be some reward for all the effort in writing poetry?

For me, it's become like deep analysis. When I start thinking of a poem somehow my synapses connect and lead me to a place where I don't normally wander into. I know a poem works if it surprises me, if I discover something. The same thing happens over and over, and I always feel a sense of release and almost intense joy for a moment when that happens. Because I know that even if the poem never gets published, even if no one else ever reads it, it has shown me something. The discoveries are not earthshaking. They're discoveries that most people make if they lead examined lives over a long period of time. If you can make them into universal discoveries, then they become art.

BK: Is there a similar process in writing a novel?

It's a similar process but not as intense. I think that the poem is the hardest thing to write. That's why when people ask me to talk about writing I always talk about the poem. It's like comparing brain surgery to any other surgery. Both operations are difficult, but one requires the skill of a diamond cutter. For me, writing a novel is a long commitment to a project and writing the poem is a rush of energy. Even though I revise the poem extensively and sometimes don't let it go for a year, it's still working with the minute. With a novel, you can delete a hundred pages and it can stand that. The patient won't die. With a poem, you can revise it into oblivion or you cannot revise it enough, and it's never quite clear to you whether you have or not.

BK: Which writers have served as models for you?

When I'm addressing a Latino audience and they ask me about models I pause because I know that they want me to say that my models were Puerto Rican writers. I can't say that. Because if you're talking about the models that formed me as an artist twenty years ago, well, there was no big multicultural drive in the United States, there were no Latino studies, nothing like it. In fact, when I was in graduate school, studying American and British literature was the only way that I could do what I wanted to do. Spanish literature from Spain did not represent my interests as closely as did American literature. My only model was Virginia Woolf, because she was the only woman who was allowed on the syllabus. But I didn't feel the shock of recognition until I happened to take a course in Southern literature where I encountered the work of Flannery O'Connor and Eudora Welty. I realized that these were women writing about ordinary lives that they had transformed through art. They weren't rich British women who could be counted among the world's Dead Englishman geniuses; these were women who were writing about family, land, religion. I would say Flannery O'Connor was the first one to give me that jolt, and years later, Alice Walker. Then followed Toni Morrison, because once you get into that era, then African-American and other people start publishing. But it wasn't until Gabriel García Márquez won the Nobel Prize and the so-called Latin American literary boom, when other Latin American writers were "discovered" by American publishers, that we then got Isabel Allende and other people in translation. It's been a long road. Now I do seek out and read the works of Puerto Rican women on the island.

I had one young person ask, "Was Sandra Cisneros your model?" I had to say, "She is a few years younger than I am!" We started publishing around the same time, she and Julia Alvarez and I. Esmeralda tells me that she used *Silent Dancing* as a model for when she began writing, so I'm already at that stage where my work is being used as a model! I have had the distinction, if one can call it that, of having been one of the original Puerto Rican writers writing in English, as opposed to being translated, or Latina writers in English. I had to make do, and it hasn't hurt me. I find that I can put into my work many things because I'm aware of the mainstream and have studied contemporary literature by all writers, not just limiting myself to Latino studies, because I think a writer needs to absorb everything.

JH: Your situation sounds like it's in harmony with Chicana writers like Cisneros and Viramontes who were reading a variety of authors as well.

Right, because we didn't have other people. And I think that it's wonderful to have African-American studies and Latino studies, but there's also an inherent danger in that if we're going to create a new generation of writers these studies need to be more interdisciplinary. These writers have to be aware of people like Cormac McCarthy and other fabulous writers who are changing the English language. How can we be innovators if we don't see what's being changed?

In my classes I teach American literature, which includes Cisneros and Gary Soto and Joy Harjo. The Library of Congress defines as an American writer a person writing in English within the boundaries of the United States who's an American citizen. So we're not minority writers, we are American writers who happen to belong to ethnic minorities. I've taught English for almost twenty years from instructor to professor now. My love is literature in all its forms by all its practitioners. But they always have to meet the criteria of excellence that I learned early to apply. I don't teach anyone because it's politically correct. I teach only those writers whose work I can justify to my students.

BK: Any examples you care to mention of what's politically correct that you refuse to teach?

No! I don't think I want to do that. I think that that would be very offensive to people out there. I would really just rather concentrate on the positive. The publishers are at fault in many ways because if a book becomes a best-seller or there's a popular trend to publish a particular kind of writer, then all of the sudden we have five books by five writers that are supposed to be like the other one. They'll say, "If you've read and loved so and so, you will love so and so." I don't think, for example, that you can compare Alice Walker to Terrie McMillan. You know what I mean? They're just completely different!

JH: Is there a difference for you between Maxine Hong Kingston and Amy Tan?

Well, those two I have a little more trouble with because I enjoy Amy Tan tremendously. But Maxine Hong Kingston was a crucial writer for me to read. She was an innovator, someone who did something completely new. Basically I really have to admire and love an artist's work and be able to justify it as literature before I teach it in my classes. But fortunately there are so many good writers out there representing so many different groups that I have no problem coming up with a very varied syllabus.

JH: Do you see yourself as a mentor for younger writers?

Yes, I do. Some of my graduate students spend four or five years under my tutelage. I end up spending a lot of personal time with them, and I don't mind it. These are extremely intelligent people, and some of them are very talented writers. Not all will have a successful future as writers, but I don't know that when I first meet them so they all get the same treatment. So, yes, I do see myself as a mentor, and as far as teaching, I knew I wanted to be a teacher before I knew I wanted to be a writer. I never thought of another career. Teaching is just what I always wanted to do ever since I was a child.

JH: What motivated you to publish poetry?

Actually there's never a great deal of encouragement to publish poetry. There's no money in it, you have to want to do it. At first, no one wanted to publish my poems for the same reason that they later wouldn't publish *The Line of the Sun*. A letter from a university press said that they liked my poems, but they used too much Spanish and their audience was not necessarily bilingual. I wondered if T. S. Eliot expected everyone to speak ancient Hindu when they read *The Wasteland*. Or whether Pound expected people to know Chinese. It didn't make sense. I sent it to Arte Público, and they took it and the next one to the Bilingual Press. At that time those were my only options because I was writing poems that contained a little Spanish, which I don't think interferes with understanding.

BK: Now the use of Spanish is more acceptable.

Exactly. It should always have been acceptable. If people care enough to read poetry, they care enough to look up a word. I went around with a bunch of dictionaries when I was reading American and British literature. Anyway, it's been a long road, and with me it hasn't exactly been like it has with Esmeralda and Sandra. My work, for whatever reason, has had to first find a home with the smaller university presses, and then, usually after it gets good reviews and awards, a big press like Penguin or Norton will pick it up. My agent just has one phrase that she uses about my work, "It is too literary." And I say, "What the hell does that mean?" It is not that it is hard to understand, it is just that it deals with subjects that are not easily translated into the mass media in some cases. I have been more fortunate recently in that my work has gotten into all the big anthologies, Norton, Oxford, that sort of thing. Now people seem a little more willing to take a chance. Norton published the paperback of the *Deli* and Penguin published the paperback of *An Island Like You*.

BK: Why do your works rely on oral histories? What's special about the oral quality of Puerto Rican literature for you?

I think that many cultures have that oral quality. In fact, my husband is a Southerner and comes from a storytelling family. But they tell their stories differently. There are certain stories that define a family and certain keywords that call them up and everyone knows that if you say something about someone or something in front of his grandmother, that she will immediately tell that story. And even though she usually tells it in the same way, it's expected and everyone enjoys it. What my grandmother liked to do that made her, at least I thought, different and unique was that she didn't mind changing the story for her audience. So I would hear her tell one story for my aunts in a particular way and assure us that it was absolutely true and then tell it to us in a different way to make a different point. What I learned about art from her was that it wasn't so much the facts as the poetic truth that was being made. I thought that was a great lesson to learn. She made an art out of stories that could've been just simple gossip. My mother and the women in the United States told stories to comfort themselves in their loneliness, to remember the island. I remember parties in the apartment in Paterson where people would actually start out telling a funny story and end up crying because the last time they heard it had been from their mothers. Storytelling is used in a culture to preserve its memories and to teach lessons for the same reason that artists write their stories. I give credit to the women in my family for giving me that lesson and some of the original stories that I used.

BK: It seems that you've also adopted your grandmother's view that when you tell a story it's for poetic truth.

Right. Absolutely. I have that little epigraph from Emily Dickinson that says, "Tell all the truth but tell it slant." I basically feel that unless I'm writing an essay where I am bound to stick to the genealogical and historical truth, I'm using my powers as a poet and an artist to compose a picture. My art is not representational but impressionistic. I like for my canvases to coalesce into meaning rather than just try to get it all photographically correct. In *Silent Dancing*, for example, I vowed to tell as much of the truth as I could. I think that book has meant a lot to some people because I think I captured the truth about what it was to be a Puerto Rican girl in the sixties. But I could not vouch that words that my grandmother had spoken back in 1960 were exactly what I had put down on the paper all these years later, so I told the poetic truth. I think that the contract with the reader is what matters as long as you let the reader know that you're working as a poet rather than a historian.

BK: At the end of *Silent Dancing* you describe your concept of truth versus fiction. Was that to protect your poetic truth?

I put that there to be fair. When I started writing *Silent Dancing* I got quite interesting responses from people. I went back to Puerto Rico and started collecting some memories, and my mother and other people would say, "No, no, that's not exactly right." So I did a little experiment. I asked different people separately to tell me the same story, my grandmother, my brother, my mother, and I remembered it and recorded it and showed it to my mother and said, "Everybody has a different version." The reason my brother's version is different is because he is male, he wasn't always in the same scenes that captured my imagination. When I was there with the women, my grandmother was concerned with running a household, my mother was concerned with keeping us safe, my aunts were thinking of something else. So the same day that we were all there thinking we were experiencing the same thing, we were all actually being the usual eyewitness, which is to say, mostly unreliable. Only the camera could have recorded it. I didn't write *Silent Dancing* as a camera, I wrote it as a poet. But I was also careful to write that preface about it not being canned memories, and then I wrote the epilogue where I say that there are people who disagree with this, but this is my version.

BK: Why did you settle on *Silent Dancing* as the title for your collection of memoirs?

One of my main obsessions and motifs is the island, the isolation of everyone being an island and how isolated you are when you don't know the language. I chose *Silent Dancing* mainly because it went well with the idea of the silent movie and I thought it was both poignant and slightly absurd to see people dancing without music. To me that had symbolic meaning for the life of the immigrant. We are trying to re-create island life in a hostile environment. That's a crucial essay for me because it reflected the sort of sad paradox of the Puerto Rican in the city.

BK: I was reminded of Charlie Chaplain, the silent movie star, but also because his movies, though funny, are also poignant and sad.

That's an interesting comparison because that's exactly what I was after. These people trying so hard to enjoy themselves and hiding behind this frivolity, which, when you see it years later, you see that it's a sort of frantic and desperate attempt to recapture something.

BK: Why do you feel the memoir is so popular now?

I think because people, due to the spirit of the times, are very interested in finding out how their fellow human beings perceive the world. There was a time when escapist literature, or travel writing, did that. I really feel that it's a reflection of our times. I read *Angela's Ashes*, for example, and was enchanted by it. It's the memoir of an Irish-American. I loved it and it was funny and it taught me something that I already knew but was glad to hear: that most poor people feel the same way about things. I think people are trying to find comfort in our common ground, and the memoir helps to do that. I think there's a reaction against the tell-all victim memoir. Like *The Kiss* or these things where people reveal their most intimate and sometimes nonuniversal aspects of themselves. Because we all know that there is incest out there, but we really don't want to know that some people get into it. We want to acknowledge it, but I don't think we want it in our face. I believe there's a strong need for a spiritual connection that the memoir may be helping us to feel. Like *The Color of Water,* about a man paying tribute to his white mother. That's unusual and I want to read it. Why shouldn't a black man love his white mother? So we want to read things that confirm that yes, we are doing the right thing, that it's O.K. to have all these different strange people around us, that we all have a common humanity. I think that may be why the memoir is important and why we are going against that tell-all, self-indulgent victim memoir. I think if anybody was a victim, Frank McCourt was a victim of society and injustice, but he managed to find his humanity in it.

BK: How autobiographical is *The Line of the Sun*?

There are a lot of autobiographical elements in it, but a lot of it is strictly fictional. Actually I had an uncle who was called Gúzman. He was the wild son who drove everybody to distraction, but everybody loved him. I used his spirit to inform that character. He died two years ago of throat cancer, and he knew that I had based my novel on him. But he also knew that it was heavily fictionalized, because, for example, I wasn't going to call my uncle and ask him about his sex life. And there was no such woman as Rosa. I made her up. She is a composite of many people. And, of course, my father was in the navy and Rafael was in the navy, and my mother has some of the same characteristics as Ramona, but there was no fire in our building, no strike that I participated in, and that sort of thing. The novel was a story I wanted to tell using the elements that I knew were possible in the barrio. It is true in that way. Everything in there was researched. Everything from the plant life to the politics of the era.

BK: And Edna Acosta-Belén, the important Puerto Rican critic, helps you with your research?

Yes. Edna, my fellow hormiguereña, is from my hometown. No one knows my work as well as Edna. She is my compatriot, my compañera, and also a woman who knows so much about the Puerto Rican woman because she has written scholarly texts about it. She's one of the original founders of Latino studies at SUNY [State University of New York]. I've always had respect for the work of the scholar and the researcher. She contributes greatly by reading my work with respect and telling me honestly, this didn't happen quite like that, or read this book or these articles. I don't want to read a book where I find out later something I thought I knew about the culture turned out to be inaccurate. Who possesses more knowledge about a culture than people who spend their lives researching it? My novels don't go out before they pass through Edna. I don't send anything out that a Puerto Rican kid may read and think is historical truth. I make up personal things, but if something happened in 1963 it has to be confirmable. The University of Georgia Press has been very good about that. For example, they had me calling the Department of the Army to find out whether the troops were integrated in 1951 because I had a black soldier [in my book]. And I consulted with the National Forest Service to make sure that all my plants and trees were flowering at the right time. You can't have somebody read about a flower coming up in Puerto Rico in June and then find that it doesn't happen. That's embarrassing. My idea of writing is to use the research skills that I practiced and acquired as a scholar with my imaginative skills.

I also have a dear friend, Rafael Ocasio, who teaches Spanish at Agnes Scott College. I just e-mailed him and said I'm thinking about botánicas and he immediately sent me two articles about botánicas. I'm also grateful to my translator, Elena Olazagasti-Segovia of Vanderbilt University, who did *Bailando en silencio* and *La línea del sol*. I feel like I'm rich. How can I not be grateful for that? I myself am not a scholar in that way, but I do a lot of research. Maybe that's why my work has caught on with the academy in some way, because people know how careful I am in constructing my text. I want to tell a very interesting story, but I also want it to be accurate and well researched. My colegas are in my acknowledgments always.

JH: How do you see your role as a writer contributing to American literature?

If I've made a contribution it's been to broaden the understanding of our group by saying that though some of us do sound like Pedro Pietri, not all of us do. I don't belong to the Nuyorican school, even though some people want to include me in it. And I have no problem with that, but I didn't grow up in New York and I don't write in the same language. I don't use Spanglish the way they do. I remember once when Nick Kanellos, the publisher of Arte Público Press, was introducing me and said, "There are the Nuyorican writers and there are the island writers and there is Judith Ortiz Cofer." I did a reading in Madison, Missouri, at Kenyon College and there were Puerto Ricans everywhere. These people see in my work a reflection of a broader diaspora. It used to be that either you were in New York or Puerto Rico. Now we are everywhere. And also I think I've contributed in the sense that my work encompasses a little more than mainstream consciousness.

BK: Reflecting back on your childhood, in *Silent Dancing* you describe the constant traveling between Puerto Rico and New Jersey and how unsettling that was. Do you think that you write to somehow create the permanence you didn't have as a child?

I don't know whether my difficult childhood propelled me to be a writer. It certainly led me to become a reader because I was lonely a lot of the time and books provided a stable, secure medium for me to return to time and again. There might be a cause and effect there. It was very difficult because I was always the new kid and children crave one set of friends and an unchanging environment in which to thrive. I do see it as my material and as an enriching experience. But when I was living it I didn't. But now I've accepted that as part of my life. For example, I'm the only Puerto Rican English teacher at the University of Georgia. There are Latina teachers in Romance Languages but I'm the only Puerto Rican English professor.

I think that if one has the desire to write, and I don't know whether it's a desire or an inclination that is innate, one finds one's vocation no matter what. I've been a writer for over twenty years, and I've met hundreds of writers from all walks of life. Some have had wonderful childhoods, like Eudora Welty, and she found things to write about. And others have had miserable childhoods, like Jim Grimsley, who wrote *Winter Birds*, a fantastic book about growing up in dire poverty in the South. He called himself the poster boy for misery. When my father first joined the U.S. Navy he had to be gone for months at a time. He was away in Panama when I was born. My mother, many of those years, chose to go back and stay at my grandmother's house in Puerto Rico. People have said that my father is a great absence in my books, and I always respond that he was a very powerful absence in my life. We didn't have the security of a father at home all the time, which is why I grew up in a matriarchal situation in Puerto Rico. For quite a few years we lived part of the year in the United States and part of the year in Puerto Rico. When we went to Puerto Rico we spoke with a different accent. In New Jersey we were on the outside and in Puerto Rico we were also on the outside. Although we had a lot of love and support from our family, the social situation was always a little strained.

JH: How does it feel to be the only Puerto Rican English teacher?

It feels the same as my life has always felt. I was the only Puerto Rican English major at my college twenty years ago, and so I adjust. I've always sort of depended on my intelligence. I let people judge me however they want, and then I always figure that I can compete. That's not arrogance. When I was in high school I always thought, well, they can think whatever they want of me but I'm going to get an A on this test. It's the same at the college here where I'm sure that some people resent that I've been successful even by their standards. But then there are others who support me and know I'm a good teacher. I don't go around feeling like a stranger because it's become so much a part of my mode and my persona and my daily existence to be the one who looks or speaks different.

I don't see it as a burden as I did when I was a child because I don't suffer from the same intense insecurities and identity problems.

BK: Do your readers demand a certain Puerto Ricanness from you?

Yes, they really do. When I go places I'm supposed to know about the political status of Puerto Rico, the history, the geography. Of course, I try and keep up. But my main message in my books is that a lifetime is an ongoing process and that evolution doesn't have to always equal progress, but it's inevitable culturally. My daughter is living in a different world than I lived in, and she will be a different kind of woman. I think that's what happens with these trends, what the country adopts right now, where we are in a frenzy where we are trying to pigeonhole people. I don't think that's going to work. When kids talk to me about that I tell them to define themselves and what they feel themselves to be first and then to go back and see what they have adapted from each culture and how much of it they actually need.

BK: What's your relationship to the island now? Do you return as a visitor to the past, or do you feel that you're returning home?

Well, that is the question, isn't it? When people ask me what are you and they mean where do you come from, I always say I'm Puerto Rican, which is obviously what I am. But I think that culture is a very complex concept. You could say that I am Puerto Rican by birth. I certainly enjoy and appreciate my heritage, and have used a lot of my culture for my art and incorporated it into my life. But then there are larger elements to living such as economics and politics and employment and sexual roles and that sort of thing. I'm culturally an American woman and a native Puerto Rican. My mother is a Puerto Rican who never became culturally an American woman. She's never happier than when she is on the island doing the things that she thinks are familiar and are her way of life, which is very different from me. I love going to the island, but it's no longer as familiar to me as Georgia. So, at the risk of sounding like I am betraying my ethnicity, when I go there I have to be more aware. It's like if you stop driving for years you become more aware of driving. It's not automatic anymore. When I go to Puerto Rico I act as when I go to Europe; I spend a lot of time observing and making sure that I know what's going on. Whereas here I'm on automatic pilot a lot of the time. For better or worse, I'm no longer the same kind of puertorriqueña that my mother is. I refuse to be politically correct and say that I'm a pure, unadulterated, native puertorriqueña. No. I've undergone an evolutionary process as has everyone who has ever left their homeland.

(9)

A Puerto Rican Existentialist in Brooklyn

An Interview with Esmeralda Santiago

Born in 1948 in Santurce, Puerto Rico, Esmeralda Santiago moved with her family to Brooklyn, New York, at the age of thirteen. Of all the women included in this book, she is the most practical about the craft of writing. Between lecturing and touring, she makes appointments with herself to write without waiting for inspiration—something, she says, she cannot trust will happen. Santiago said that her writing process evolved in self-defense from the demands of her life and the struggle of trying to write with two small children. Now, though her children are older, she still schedules writing time. She also told of how reading literature, especially Jean Paul Sartre and Simone de Beauvoir, saved her during her adolescent years in the United States. "I was the only Puerto Rican girl I knew who was an existentialist in Brooklyn," she says. She believes that a certain part of existentialism, the sense of "just having to take it as it comes," helped her to keep moving forward.

Santiago did not realize that she wanted to become a writer until her first child was born and she began to write short essays about herself and growing up in Puerto Rico just for fun, never expecting them to get published. At that point in her life she wrote because she had something to say. Much to her surprise, the essays were published first in her local newspaper in Hingham, Massachusetts, and later in newspapers like the Boston Globe. Santiago's essays date back to the early eighties and have appeared in newspapers rang-

ing from the New York Times *to the* Christian Science Monitor. *These nonfiction essays are microcosms of the themes that preoccupy her and appear in her later works. She deals with themes such as identity. For example, "A Puerto Rican Stew," published in the* New York Times Magazine, *tells of finding a recipe for her own identity. Other essays deal with the plight of empleadas, life in the barrios of New York, motherhood, and island politics.*

Santiago completed her B. A. at Harvard University and her M.F.A. at Sarah Lawrence, where her thesis project was her memoir, When I Was Puerto Rican *(1993). The memoir depicts Santiago's early years on the island and ends with her acceptance into New York's Performing Arts High School. She also published* América's Dream *(1996), a novel about the struggle of a Puerto Rican woman who moves to New York to work as a live-in nanny for an American family. In 1999 the sequel to* When I Was Puerto Rican, *titled* Almost a Woman, *which has won three awards from the American Library Association, was published. She also edited, along with Joie Davidow,* Las Christmas *(1998), an anthology of Christmas memoirs by Latinos across the nation and* Las Mamis *(2000), an anthology in honor of Latina mothers. Santiago lives in Westchester County, New York, with her husband and two children.*

B.K.

BK: Is it hard keeping an appointment with yourself when you're not in the mood?

If I have the time, I'm in the mood. I don't trust inspiration because you can't count on it. If I say that I'm going to write at nine o'clock on Monday, then I'm there writing. Very rarely will I get into one of these Oh, but I'm not inspired funks, because I don't have the luxury. I'm more of a workman type of writer. I have something to say, and I work hard to say it. But I also have a husband and children and a full life that I participate in. I don't obsess over writing. It's not a painful process for me as it is for some writers I know, who really suffer if they can't get inspired. I suffer because I'd like to do it more. Now that's becoming more possible as my life changes, my children grow, and I'm able to structure my time better. The actual process of writing is difficult and emotionally draining, but I don't feel that it's torture. It's just my job, and one I like to do. But when I finish writing, that's it. I go on to my next event. I might go to the movies with my husband, or to my son's lacrosse game, or I have to cook dinner, or my daughter has to be driven to the mall because her life depends on a new outfit. I guess I compartmentalize my life so that I can keep it all straight.

BK: Which is something characteristic of women who have to switch roles.

That's right. We don't have the luxury to wallow in angst. Some writers who have less complicated lives seem unhappy because they can't get away from the process of writing, from the words and from the emotion they're putting out day after day. I don't have the luxury of writing all the time, but I do have a very full life and I'm able to get away from the writing and do other things that keep me sane. Some days when I say to myself that I have to write at nine o'clock and I get up and don't feel like writing, and of course that happens, I still say to myself, if you don't write today you're not going to be able to write for another week, so get to it. It's a question of priorities, and of taking control of the process, rather than letting the process control me.

BK: On a technical note, do you know your endings first, your characters, your plot?

Well, it's real easy when I'm writing a memoir! I know where to start and where I'm going next. I also have a pretty good idea of where I would *like* it to end. It's basically plotted in my mind because I was there and know what happened. When I'm working on a memoir, I note down everything I can remember, whether it's going to make it into the final draft or not. I try not to edit as I go along because I never know where a particular memory of an event or person will take me. Basically I trust that if I remember it, it's important. I follow the process of memory, which is sometimes chronological but often has its own needs. Once I have it all down, I'll go to the library and check dates of historical events, listen again to music from the period I'm writing about, to get a renewed sense of what the cultural environment around me was like. Even in that note-taking phase I let memory guide me. For example, I won't research the drug culture of 1967 because I wasn't a part of it. Or if I was, I don't remember it!

I also develop an outline. For a memoir, I write a bunch of dates and key things that I remember happening in a particular year, even though most of the time I don't refer to the outline. But the process of setting it down "toggles" the imagination. If I get stuck or if I get to my office and don't feel like writing, then I consult the outline and say to myself, well, let's see, last time I was writing about 1967, and that gets me going.

With fiction, I write an actual beginning-to-end narrative outline with character sketches, sample scenes, and a middle and an end as I see it. I try to get as close to what the finished story will be. Like the nonfiction outline, I don't necessarily consult it that much, but it's there to help me if I get stuck. Because I don't write every day, I need a blueprint so that I don't get lost or discouraged.

BK: Is one genre harder than the other for you to write?

It's all hard. When I'm writing a memoir I can't wait to be done so that I can write fiction, and when I'm writing fiction I think it's so much easier to write a memoir. It's all a challenge. One would think that a memoir would be easier because you were there, but the responsibilities are quite different from writing fiction, where you can make it all up. In memoir the responsibilities are to what happened, to what you experienced. I think writers constantly fool themselves into thinking that the next book will be easier!

BK: Do you think that women write differently than men?

Yes I do. I often wonder what the *Odyssey* would be about if it had been written from the point of view of Penelope. I'm sure that in all the time that Odysseus was gone, she did more than weave a shroud and complain about the suitors. Her loneliness, her longing, her single parenthood are as worthy of being explored in song and poetry as Odysseus's journey. Because of the way that story was told, I'm convinced Homer wasn't a woman!

I also think that, by and large if you really study it, you'll find that there's a distinct use of language based on gender and on what tasks characterize your life. Women writers are more likely to use the metaphors of cooking, sewing, cleaning, nurturing, and taking care of people and things. That's not to say that men don't do it as well, they just don't do it as often.

I take advantage of that difference. If I'm going to find an image, I'll deliberately go to the more traditional female occupations. I love all the needle arts, embroidery, tejer, knitting, and weaving. And even though for centuries it was the man who was the weaver, in our culture it's more frequently the women who do that work. So I use that language even though I have access to metaphors that may be more related to my every-day life. I don't weave! But I love the whole metaphorical implications of weaving.

BK: Who were some of your models when you were growing up and reading?

Until the age of thirteen I was educated in Puerto Rico, so my influences were mostly the island poets Luis Pales Matos, Luis Llorens Torres, los grandes. There was also an emphasis on Latin American poets like Sor Juana, Gabriela Mistral, and Rubén Darío and his generation of poets. In Spanish-speaking countries that's our education. I didn't read Emily Dickinson until I came to the States. When I came to New York and made it my business to learn English, I read everything I could get my hands on. At that time I wanted to find stories about teenagers, about young people who were going through the same kinds of things that I was going through. I read *Auntie Mame, Daddy Long Legs, The Diary of Anne Frank, A Tree Grows in Brooklyn, The Heart Is a Lonely Hunter*. I loved Carson McCullers. I read everything I could by Cornelia Otis Skin-ner. In the process of reading these books about young people, I discov-ered that I didn't exist in the literature of the United States. There were no books about Puerto Rican girls in Brooklyn. I think that I was driven to be a writer because I didn't exist in the literature, and therefore didn't exist in the culture. I simply wasn't there. Later I started reading more heady work. I went through a long period where I read everything that Jean Paul Sartre and Simone de Beauvoir wrote. I was the only Puerto Rican girl I knew who was an existentialist in Brooklyn. I went through everything I could get my hands on of that literature. Maybe that's why I was so depressed!

It's always really hard for me to say who my influences are because I'm such an avid reader. It's hard for me to say that Gabriel García Márquez influenced me more than Jane Austen. Or Jane Austen more than George Eliot or George Eliot more than Mario Vargas Llosa. It's not that way at all. I get what I can from everyone I read. With the possible exception of Dickens, I think I've read all the classics and all the modern icons. For a writer, everything you read contributes to your craft and to give more weight to one writer or another is unfair unless you're deliberately trying to write like, say, Hemingway.

BK: Why did Sartre and de Beauvoir strike such a chord in you?

It was the sense of having to take life as it comes. As a teenage girl in Brooklyn I had no power. I figured that one way of giving myself power was to adopt the attitude that this is life and to just acknowledge it. Either you can get really depressed and decide to commit suicide or you can say this is the way things are and just keep moving forward. I think that that aspect of existentialism really appealed to me. You basically assume that things will go wrong and life is suffering and you just accept that, and once you accept that, it's very freeing. Whenever good things happen you're really surprised, and, though few and far between, you accept them and are happy, but then you continue moving forward. That's really what attracted me to that whole school of thought.

I never got into the American classics. I've never read *Little Women*. I never liked that kind of Pollyannaish the-sun-will-come-out-tomorrow kind of thing. Because my reality was that the sun didn't come out and that it was going to rain and I was going to get wet. And I'd just have to accept that. I think Sartre and de Beauvoir saved my life, because if I hadn't found something that I could relate to in my own life, well, who knows what would've happened. I'm sure that it was their writing that kept me sane in my adolescence.

BK: Your memoir does not have a "sun-will-come-out-tomorrow" tone. Even the title deals with a difficult reality for Puerto Ricans in the United States. Can you talk about the reactions to *When I Was Puerto Rican?*

When I first went to Puerto Rico I had to explain the title because people were defensive about what the past tense signifies. I explained that I know, value, and celebrate my Puerto Rican identity but that in the United States

I'm called Hispanic or Latina. I'm denied my very specific Puerto Rican identity for political expediencies. If the terms "Hispanic" and "Latina" did not exist, our leaders would have a hard time conveying the sheer numbers of our population. I understand and respect the need for an all-encompassing term for descendants of Spanish-speaking América. I also know that fashions change and that, while Hispanic was en vogue for a while and now Latina is en vogue, one of these days another term will be developed to convey the same reality and political necessity.

I am, however, and always will be Puerto Rican, no matter how many other labels are placed on me. When I explained this in Puerto Rico, people understood a bit more. I also made sure I described that when I returned to Puerto Rico after twelve years of living in the United States, Boricuas on the island told me I was no longer Puerto Rican because I had lived afuera for so long. I didn't feel welcome. I felt como que me fuí. Pero, I hadn't left, I'd been taken from Puerto Rico. I had no choice about it. I was brought to the United States, and once here, I did everything that was expected from me and tried not to embarrass Puerto Ricans in any way. When I went back to Puerto Rico I felt totally unwelcome because I'd had this experience outside the island. I was all of a sudden persona non grata. I didn't feel like fighting that. At least in the United States, if I tell people I'm Puerto Rican they don't say, No, you're not! I'm not going to live in an environment where I constantly have to defend my identity because I've already had to do that once in my life and I'm not going to do it at this late age.

It was devastating to be denied an identity I had struggled so hard to uphold. It was especially difficult to understand why my own people challenged my sense of a self that was the only source of comfort when things were rough. When I titled my book in the past tense, I was answering those who disputed my right to call myself Puerto Rican—You said I was not Puerto Rican enough for you. Read this book. Tell me this is not a Puerto Rican experience.

I was also trying to begin a dialogue about the degrees of Puertoricanness on the island, which I think are destructive and divisive. How can we ever solve the problems we have as a people if we bicker about who is more Puerto Rican and who is less? And who is a "real" Puerto Rican? "Real" as opposed to what? Against whom are we measuring ourselves? The past tense in the title of my book is an attempt to provoke Puerto Ricans into examining what we mean when we call ourselves

Puerto Rican. I, a Puerto Rican living in the United States, feel as Puerto Rican as if I'd never left the island. And yet there is the question of my North American life, my North American husband, my North American children. Does that make me less Puerto Rican than Norma, my younger sister? She was born three years after me, lived in New York for seven years, returned to Puerto Rico, and has lived there her entire adult life. She is English/Spanish bilingual. Does her New York experience make her less Puerto Rican than her sons, who have never lived in the United States?

I know that the book is taught in Puerto Rico and that it's part of the dialogue about our history and our cultural identity. I'm proud to have contributed something to that dialogue, but it's painful when people question the identity you've forged.

BK: What do you think motivates that kind of questioning of what seems an obvious fact, que tú eres puertorriqueña?

Because of their own feeling of inadequacy, of allowing what has happened in Puerto Rico to have happened. When I defended myself in Puerto Rico, I would say, "Look, you say I'm Americanized. Well, I have an excuse. I've lived in the United States for twelve years. But you have no excuse for being as American as you are because you stayed in Puerto Rico and you allowed McDonald's and Burger King. You allowed American culture to overwhelm Puerto Rican culture. So you can't accuse me of being Americanized and then defend yourself as less so, because I see something different." I think it's that feeling of guilt for allowing our culture to become completely diluted, contaminated. And it's a contamination that just gets worse and worse. The language, our lifestyle, the foods we choose to eat, the medicines we take, the music we listen to, the clothes we wear. It's at a very deep level. American culture has swallowed much of Puerto Rican culture. But many Puerto Ricans aren't willing to admit that.

BK: Did you worry about telling the truth in *When I Was Puerto Rican*?

I start from the point of view that I'm going to be as honest as I possibly can and I'm going to tell what I remember without interpreting it because I think the process of memory itself is interpretive. So I say to myself this is what I remember, it's as truthful and honest an accounting as I can summon and have the skills to set down. After I write it I begin to worry about whether I should be concerned with other people's reactions.

My family has been incredibly generous about accepting my version of my life. So I'm not so much worried about them as I am about other kinds of reactions. For example, I have a relative who figures prominently in the memoirs that I'm now writing. She was involved in a very dangerous, abusive relationship for a number of years, and after she left the relationship, the man stalked her. For years now she has been living in a different state from the rest of her family, under an assumed name, a life under siege, because a man she loved and trusted misused his power. I have an obligation to protect this person, and so she will not figure in my book, even though she was there, in my life.

BK: Domestic violence is an important theme in *América's Dream*.

It's something that's important to me because people close to me have been involved in abusive situations. I would like to do my bit to bring attention to the problem of domestic violence and to the many different aspects of it. I think it's something that is oversimplified. It's something that I want to keep exploring because I think it's a very, very big issue in our contemporary lives and it's getting worse, not better.

BK: Another important theme in this book is giving voice to the empleadas.

If I were to review my past as a writer, and perhaps because I am not a writer of inspiration but a writer of craft, I think my task is to give voice to people who don't have the skill, ability, time, or craziness that I have. My characters will always be those people who can't speak for themselves. I was a child who could not find myself in the literature. There was no one telling my story. I don't want that to ever happen to any child or any woman. To really see yourself as nonexistent is the worst kind of insult that a person can have. It's one thing to feel that you don't belong, we all feel that at one time or another. But there's a whole segment of our population, of our humanity, that feels like they don't exist. That's what I felt when I came to the United States. Patrick Dennis exists with his *Auntie Mame* and Carson McCullers's characters exist, and the kids in *A Tree*

Grows in Brooklyn exist, the Irish exist, but Puerto Rican girls in Brooklyn don't exist, Puerto Rican girls who are poor don't exist.

BK: You spoke with many empleadas for this novel. What's the biggest concern they expressed?

The biggest theme for them is feeling unappreciated and undervalued. For example, in one of the scenes América is cleaning out one of the closets and she finds that her employer spends more for a pair of shoes than she spends on her salary. This is something that I heard and still hear from the empleadas. It's amazing how much money is spent on things that are luxuries, but this necessity, this person on whom you depend, is not valued as highly as a pair of shoes. That was a real story that I heard from an empleada, and I thought that I should put it in the book. When América goes to ask for a raise, she is rejected in no uncertain terms. Yet América sees that this woman will drop thirty dollars on a pair of panties. Is there justice in that?

When people talk to me about *América's Dream*, a lot of American women say, "Oh my God, you really made me think twice about the way I treat my empleada." Others are insulted because they think I've been hard on them. But by and large, the majority of women's responses has been that I treated them both so fairly. It's hard to say that I'm on América's or Karen Leverett's side. They see Karen Leverett's dilemma. It's interesting that everyone finds what they need in it. As a writer, that's great, because I think the ambiguity is a big part of the relationship empleadas have with their employers and vice versa.

BK: The relationship between América and Karen is interesting. Essentially, Karen is as lonely as América.

Right. And yet they couldn't share their loneliness. Karen would not have wanted to know about América's problems. It has to be that way so that the employer doesn't feel guilty about it. She must maintain the illusion that América is part of the family. That is the other thing that I hear from the empleadas. They say, "I have problems, concerns, and feelings and they are never addressed. If you look sad one morning, they do everything they can to avoid engaging you in what is really wrong."

BK: Why did you take the time to translate your works instead of writing new material?

When the issue was first brought to me about translating *When I Was Puerto Rican* it was from the point of view, give it a try. It was more of an experiment than anything else. And the truth is that, for me, the translation is more of a rewrite. I don't do it line by line, word by word, the way a translator would. I feel I have a completely different audience in Spanish, and that even though I wrote it in English in a certain way, I might want to say it a different way in Spanish because it has more weight, or the rhythm is different, or I don't have to explain as much.

I liked doing it because it felt like I was reclaiming the Spanish that I thought I'd lost. It was a wonderful learning experience, and I'm grateful for it. But it was hard work, and I swore I'd never do it again. Then I wrote *América's Dream*, and my editor said, "We would really like you to translate it." I did it, but I didn't do a very good job. I didn't have a lot of time, wasn't given much support in the process, and didn't do it as willingly as I did for *When I Was Puerto Rican*. There were many errors in the hardcover edition, which were corrected in the paperback. But I learned my lesson. Now I'd rather the publishers find someone else to translate. I would rather keep creating, not going over the same thing.

BK: How do you choose your Spanish words?

I pay a lot of attention to the weight of words. Any word that's in Spanish in my English text is not there by accident, or because I couldn't figure out how to translate it, but rather because it has a resonance in Spanish that it doesn't have in English. Especially with value words like dignidad. With food words it's a little different because you want the flavor. But with value words I like to point out to the English-language reader that a particular word has much more weight in Spanish than it does in English. I call it coding, which is probably a term of deconstruction. I do a lot of cultural coding in my work. There are moments, phrases, expressions that resonate with a Spanish speaker, specifically a Puerto Rican, in a way that it wouldn't resonate with a non–Puerto Rican or a non-Spanish speaker. A Spanish reader brings a whole different set of experiences to the reading that the English, the American, or the Swedish reader doesn't.

BK: What do you feel about Spanglish?

Well, I happen to love Spanglish because it's the language that I use to communicate with my sisters and brothers. It gets the job done in an efficient way. As a writer I look for any opportunity to use language freely and openly. I don't believe in not allowing language to grow and to do what it needs to do. My Spanish is Puerto Rican Spanish and I'm proud of it. And if Puerto Rican Spanish is contaminated by English, well, so it is. I think when people are not able to understand one another is when we have a problem. I don't have any issues at all with Spanglish. It's the language of our young people, and there's no way that anyone is going to eradicate it unless they make everybody learn perfect castellano. Which nobody speaks except maybe in La Academia Española allá en Madrid. People who want to hold on to language and not allow it to grow are living in the past. There will come a time when we'll all speak a beautiful amalgam of all the languages of the world. Personally, I look forward to that day, although I'm certain I won't be around to experience it.

BK: How do you explain the current interest in Latina literature?

The interest was always there on the part of readers. The books weren't. Now the great thing is that these books are available. People frequently tell me, "I was looking for books like yours." They just couldn't find them. I think that publishers hadn't tapped into the potential. And yes, maybe we're the flavor of the month, but the only thing we can do is enjoy it while it lasts. We must keep writing, take advantage of the fact that publishers have finally noticed there is a market for Latino literature, and keep buying books by Latino authors, so that more and more of us get published.

I remember when Philip Roth's books first burst into the scene. Some critics said his work was "too" Jewish. And then there was talk about Jewish literature. He's still writing, and his books are selling to people who have never set foot in a synagogue. The same has been said of some of the Latino literature—that it's too specifically Latino to appeal to a broader audience. But I think if we hang in there, keep writing our books the way we want to, eventually that label will disappear, until our literature doesn't have to be labeled by our ethnicity.

BK: You call Nicholasa Mohr la madrina of Latina fiction, why?

I recognize that she's been out there a lot longer than many of us, writing her stories when no one else was paying much attention except for the enlightened teachers who used her books for their courses. It took me a long time to find her work. I wasn't familiar with Nicholasa's work until I went to Sarah Lawrence, of all places. It wasn't in my local Barnes & Noble in Hingham, Massachusetts! I think that people like Nicholasa and Piri Thomas and Rudolfo Anaya have to be commended and recognized. They were developing this literature way before some of us were born, before some of us had the courage to get our own works out there. And they did it with very little support or encouragement. They were the only ones with the courage to say these experiences are important, and we have to set them down. We have to respect that and celebrate it. We have to give them credit.

BK: What's your definition of a Latina writer?

I write in English. And that's what, in the publishing world, identifies me as a Latina writer as opposed to someone like Isabel Allende who is sometimes labeled a Latina writer, but, in fact, she writes in Spanish first. I'd guess that a Latino writer is also an American citizen with Latin American ancestry who writes about the Latin American experience in English. No one would ever call Gabriel García Márquez a Latino writer. That's the way I define it to myself.

BK: How do you distinguish yourself from a Chicana writer, for example, or any other Latina writers?

I think my writing is distinctive from Esmeralda Santiago's because it's my voice, my diction, my vocabulary, my observations. We all have access to the same language, but it's how we use that language that creates a writer's voice. There are thousands of writers who are better than I am, whose skill is greater, but it's my hope that in style and content, my work cannot be confused with Gioconda Belli's, Tato Laviera's, or Denise Chávez's.

I'm thrilled that there's such a thing as "Latino literature," and I love the fact that we are grouped together as "Latino" writers, because it lends a specificity to what we do. When I'm in a high school or in one of the forgotten colleges where our kids are studying—and I'm not talking about the big universities, but smaller places in communities devoid of Latino culture—the students often ask who else they should be reading, because in their local library the only Spanish-surnamed authors they can find are Isabel Allende or Gabriel García Márquez. I'm able to name Denise Chávez, Sandra Cisneros, Julia Alvarez, Junot Díaz, and many others. I can put all those names out there and say this is who you should be reading in your spare time. Yes, you should read Flaubert, Jane Austen, Mario Vargas Llosa, but you should also read Piri Thomas and Abraham Rodriguez because they are writing about your experience. I'm so happy when I can tell young people who are hungry to read about their lives that there is a literature that addresses their lives. I can tell them they will enjoy reading this funny mixture we have of English and Spanish, whether it's written as Spanglish or whether it's English with some Spanish words thrown in. This Latino literature, I can say to them, is written by somebody who lives the culture and is able to tap into all that implies. This Latino writer is speaking to you, and you are no longer invisible in literature. You exist in it. That, I think, is wonderful. I'm not a teacher, but in some sense I'm educating the child I was, a child who was hungry for something that did not exist and that now does exist. I want to make sure that our kids know this literature is there for them.

But it's also good when I'm compared to people like Henry Roth, the author of *Call It Sleep*. In my reviews some people compared *When I Was Puerto Rican* to *A Tree Grows in Brooklyn* and to *Call It Sleep* and to my hero Carson McCullers's work. That brings my writing to another level in which culture doesn't matter, in which it's all about being human, regardless of gender, race, ethnicity, age. The world of literature is vast. I try to stay open to all sorts of influences and possibilities for communication, and I value that a lot. I have as much in common with a writer like Ben Cheever, who is male, suburban, American born and raised, as I do with Aurora Levins Morales, because we are all in the same struggle. I like to feel that I belong in the world of writers, not just female, not just Latina, not just over fifty or under thirty! I belong in that bigger world. But other times I need to be, and insist on being, grouped with the Latinos because our people need *that*. We need to know that we have a literature of our own. William Faulkner was a male, Southern, American writer. Sometimes one or the other of those, sometimes all three. Sometimes even more adjectives could be added to describe him. But what mattered was not who he was but what his literature said.

Again, I'm a Puerto Rican writer because I'm a Puerto Rican woman and my themes are Puerto Rican life. But even if my themes were life in fourteenth-century Indonesia, I would be a Puerto Rican writer because I'm a Puerto Rican woman. In the immortal words of Popeye, "I am what I am and that's all that I am!"

(10)
Praying for Knowledge

An Interview with Helena María Viramontes

Born in East Los Angeles in 1954, Helena María Viramontes was inspired to write by listening to the stories of the women in her community. She grew up in a household of eleven where her mother always made sure that there was room for one more relative to eat and tell his story. I listened to some of these stories on a visit to her home in Ithaca, New York, in February 1998. Over red wine she reminisced about the "old days" when Chicano/Latino literature was unknown, about how she helped form writing groups, and, of course, about going out with her comadres, her girlfriends. When I entered her study, I encountered books, notes, and a nopal plant on her desk, an item that gives her spiritual substance to accompany her long hours of writing. Welcoming and open, she extended an invitation to her class on U.S. Latino/a literature at Cornell University. As Viramontes lectured on an important Nuyorican writer, Jesús Colón, the students were captivated by the power of her words, a frankness and poise she naturally conveys. While she taught, she drew in her students so that they would share their ideas and feel at ease. As a mother of two adolescents, a wife, a creative writing and literature professor, a mentor to undergraduate and graduate students, and, of course, a writer, Viramontes still has time for a meditation class, a "prayer to the world," that prepares her for the process of writing.

Viramontes has been writing and winning literary prizes since the 1970s.

She received her M.F.A. in creative writing from the University of California at Irvine, where she studied under Thomas Keneally, author of Schindler's List. *She published her first collection of stories,* The Moths and Other Stories, *in 1985, to pay tribute to her community in East Los Angeles. The stories "The Moths" and "Cariboo Cafe" have been widely anthologized. She has also collaborated with critic María Herrera-Sobek in some of the first literary anthologies of Chicana literature,* Chicana Creativity and Criticism: Charting New Frontiers in American Literature *(1987) and* Chicana (W)rites on Word and Film *(1994), both of which were inspired by academic conferences she helped to coordinate. In 1989 Viramontes participated in a storytelling workshop sponsored by the Sundance Film Institute under the guidance of Gabriel García Márquez. She wrote her first novel,* Under the Feet of Jesus *(1995), in memory of César Chávez and her parents. This work traces the struggle of migrant farmworkers in the orchards of California through female adolescent eyes. The plight of the migrant and the immigrant in America is a theme that deeply touches Viramontes. Interestingly enough, I first met her at the conference "Writing the Immigrant Experience" in 1994, which set us off on a series of conversations for the following interview.*

J.H.

JH: It's interesting that they would hold this conference, "Writing the Immigrant Experience," at the public library in downtown L.A. What does this place mean to you?

The public libraries provide special and safe spaces for the imagination, especially for a poor barrio family of eleven. I'm an outspoken advocate for public libraries because I grew up in a bookless home in East L.A. and it wasn't until my older brothers and sisters started going to school that we had books in our home. Except maybe the Bible. My sister had a Bible, and I was always amazed by the pictures. For the longest time I thought that this book held a combination of sacred words and that it contained all the truth in the world. That's all one really needs as a human being, no? It wasn't until very recently that I realized that this wasn't always the case. But that's where I developed my respect for the printed word. In any event, I was always excited about books. The library was my freedom space and I had the world at my fingertips. I would take two buses to come here.

JH: What do you remember about the library as a child?

First of all, it was a place of warmth. The heater was always on full blast, making it a welcome place especially in winter, and especially for the homeless. Nobody bothered you either. When you first entered the old L.A. Public Library, you encountered this huge room full of card catalog drawers. You could open any of them and ¡AY! como tenían tantos libros . . . the cards meant many books [she extends her hands]. Then to go to the stacks and pull them off the shelves, and then to go into a room and to sit down with them. It was glorious. Anything you wanted to know was at your disposal. There was always a homeless person or two, three, ten, either sleeping, reading, or looking at odd things like outdated TV guides for example. And nobody messed with them. The librarians or clerks left them alone. I thought that was fascinating. It's always been my quiet, tripping out space, the library. I had this feeling of ownership, that the public library belonged to me as well as everyone else.

JH: Which books captured your imagination?

Just about anything. I always enjoyed looking at encyclopedias. Biographies were just fascinating to me. I loved people like Irving Stone, who would write fictionalized versions of biographies. I also enjoyed reading about California history. I would select these items off the shelf. The old public library did have this atrium where in the center you had rows and rows of card catalogs. And I used to go nuts because I thought, where do I go first? The fact that I could look up any information in the world just amazed me. There was never enough time to read.

JH: How do you look back on your college years at Immaculate Heart?

Well, it was the first time I moved away from home and lived in a coed dorm. I was in a small four-year liberal arts college that was predominantly white. It was the first time that I was introduced to a number of fascinating feminist professors who had a marvelous education to give us. Even though the college was a Catholic institution, the nuns who taught there offered critical and opinionated tools that seemed liberating, made us students of the world. They did things out of the norm. For example, shortly after the Chicago Seven trials, they had hired Tom Hayden to teach. This was back in 1971, the time of the moratoriums, the Chicano movement, and the civil rights movement. There was a lot of excitement. At the same time, I suffered culture shock like my fellow classmates of color. We were it, basically. Yet I am deeply thankful for these radical professors who were giving us this wonderful information. I mean, I was reading the Soledad brother letters under the guise of prison writings or resistance writings. This is the type of course that is not being offered today. We also had philosophy and ethics classes on abortion, on test tube babies. They told us that these are the types of questions that we would have to face as citizens of the United States. In essence, they forced us to think in terms of the future, to think about these issues and negotiate our ethics with the rest of the world.

JH: And your parents approved of this education?

Education for females wasn't easy in our household. I was the first mujer to move out of the house. So I needed parental permission to move into a dorm. I felt I had to move out of the house in order to succeed as a student. My father said that I would move out over his dead body. I then approached my mother and basically tricked her. I asked her, "Do you want me to meet a doctor or lawyer? Where am I going to meet them if I don't go to a university where they are studying?" She immediately signed the paper. My roommate, this woman from Pacific Palisades, reminded me of Janis Joplin. She was a very wild, rebellious person. For me, it was the first time I got to know an upper-middle-class white woman my age. We had a blast together because of her outrageousness, and my courageousness to try just about anything once. When my parents visited, they kept looking for and asking about the nuns. They kept wondering where they all were. I suppose they kept picturing habit-clad nuns watching over their little angels. I kept saying that they were busy studying. Yeah, I remember those crazy, crazy days.

BK: When did you begin to write? What compels you to write?

Each story has its own genesis, be it a symbol, mood, character, voice, or emotion that first carries the story. When I first began writing shortly after college, there were several things that inspired me. One was rage. I remember raging against the patriarchal system, raging against the world and its injustices. I felt as if I had to write out of some type of under-standing of what was going on and what I was feeling. But when it came to the point that I started sharing my work with other people, they pointed out that this story was theirs as well. This character reminded them of their father or whatever. Then I realized that I was not writing person-ally about myself, but I was writing about a community of people. That's when I decided that I had to write the best that I could because I was not writing only for myself. For me, it started as a personal investment. As a literature major and a lover of great books, I also was very fascinated by the novel's storytelling and the possibilities of language and those things that captured my imagination.

JH: Which writers influenced you at this time?

In college I was reading a lot of African-American writers like Ralph El-lison. Toni Morrison came a bit later. Angela Davis had an impact on me as well. I was very impressed by that kind of radical atmosphere of writing your roots and yourself and the urban plight.

I also became interested in the Latin American writers and their works: *One Hundred Years of Solitude, Pedro Páramo*. I had been reading a lot, but this was so different from anything that I had ever read. It was so en-joyable. It was the type of reading that just drew me in. I just forgot about the hours. You get so much into something. You are immersed in it then. Oh! What a wonderful thing! I can't even describe it—to be in another world completely and not let anybody distract you from it until you are out of it. That's what I got from a lot of these Latin American writers. I was very fascinated by their technique, by their storytelling, by the way they narrated, by their information.

JH: "The Moths," your most anthologized short story, what inspired it?

The story was inspired by a photograph taken by W. Eugene Smith for *Life* magazine, I believe, and I think the title of it is "Minamata." Like all wonderful photos, this one has a story to it. It was taken to document a village struggle against mercury pollution that caused a number of birth defects. A Japanese mother bathes her nineteen-year-old child. I was overpowered by the love I saw between this mother and her deformed child. While the child looks into space, the mother shows such love and compassion in bathing the child. I felt the strength of bonding, love and trust between the two. I wanted to capture this feeling in the relationship between the grandmother and her grandchild in "The Moths." I chose the grandmother figure instead of the mother figure because she has more time to take care of the children. The mother figure is too close a generation to relate to her rebellious daughter. This story is a tribute to grandparents and the role they play in our lives. I also show in this story that these people have real lives with complexities. There are no easy solutions.

JH: "Cariboo Café" is another significant landmark in expressing the concerns of the immigrant experience. How did you become interested in this issue?

In 1984 my husband, Eloy, was doing a research project in Vancouver, British Columbia. We had just had our daughter, Pilar, who was only a few months old at the time. The Canadian newspapers, unlike those in the States, were very good about uncovering the death squads and disappearances in Central America. Except for maybe Tom Wicks of the *New York Times*, little information was being given to the American people about what was happening with the support of American dollars. I became obsessively involved with the issues and began clipping and pasting new articles. I kept an intense journal at the time thinking to myself, this is the world I'm giving to my daughter?! I wanted to scream with this story too, to make the readers part of it, witness it, bring them in. I wanted readers to be active participants, make them realize that they are bystanders in the end looking and accepting what is going on with their silence. At the same time, I wanted them to experience the pain of this woman in losing a child senselessly—a fact that was happening left and right. At times I cried as I was writing it. Other times I had nightmares about it. One night I woke up screaming because my inner motherly instincts came out again. I saw this man take my child. I was running and touching her. She was reaching out to me. I was running faster. It scared the hell out of me. I woke up screaming. I did not know the power of the story, but I felt that I needed to do something. I needed to recognize that these women were very much silenced in the United States because people were not covering this type of material.

JH: Why do you choose the fragmented form not only in that story but others as well?

As the writer, I was trying to find out the story myself, and I had to let them tell me. I've always tried to experiment with a narrative form that would be appropriate or truthful to the voices of the characters. But different people have different theories about my form. For example, Sonia Saldívar-Hull [critic of Chicana literature] writes of the "Cariboo Café" that I use that form as a way of reflecting the disenfranchised, the fragmented world, the fragmented way that these marginalized people live. Then there is a postmodern vision of that particular story again in the experimentation with narrative form. That is what I found so utterly fascinating, that people can be allowed to fragment, trying it this way and that way.

JH: I find this rebellious spirit in many of your female characters. How does this relate to your writing process?

That's right. And believe me, this is something that I am doing through my writing. That it is not something I am realizing all of a sudden. I get up and I say, "God, it was through my characters." You know it's interesting, because when I wrote to Sandra (Cisneros) and I told her, "You know, Sandra, I have to be a thankful woman for many things. But one thing I'm very thankful for is these characters: you know they gave me life." That's the way I feel. Writing is so basic and so much a part of my own development as a human being that this is what I want to offer my readers too.

JH: Actually, could you talk about Gabriel García Márquez and the Storytelling Workshop sponsored by the Sundance Institute that you attended?

First of all, he was a fascinating storyteller. Whenever he described a student, he described the characteristics of the student or a particular detail that I would remember. I learned a couple of things from that workshop. One was that I should never be satisfied with my imagination, always push it to the extent that I can with a particular thing. If you are going to have a bird in your story, why don't you give that bird characterization? Why don't you make that bird come and talk to you? Once you begin to think of that, it's a lot of fun.

And Márquez just reemphasized how much you have to love life, how much you have to love your characters and the whole fascination with storytelling, how much you have to embrace it with hope, to be able to push and believe in the imagination. It was a real enforcement to that aspect. He is such a generous man who always had kind words. He would always put his cheek down so I could kiss him in the morning. Very loving man. When we left [the workshop at the Sundance Institute], he said that there was no one who was more sentimental than he was. He had tears in his eyes. He turned around, said "So long," and walked out the door. It was crushing for us. We just sat down and cried. He is an incredibly gifted man, a great teacher.

JH: You have written scripts and worked on a film. How does that medium complement your writing of fiction?

Well, I think that after I came out of the Sundance, I thought I could write a script. If Gabo says I can write a script, I can write one. I was in complete self-denial. It took six months, a long time, to write a thirty-page script because I was workshopping myself, going back and forth to my how-to books. My script was accepted by the American Film Institute in the Women's Directing Workshop, and it was shot by the filmmaker Ana María García. The actual experience of writing that script helped me to write *Under the Feet of Jesus*. It kept my mind active in trying to tell a story in images. That's why so many people think this novel is very cinematic. In a way it reflected my experiences as a scriptwriter. It was a challenge. I got to hand it to those people who write good scripts. It's a lot harder than fiction, because in fiction you say "He felt" or "She thought." How can you translate those things into film unless you have an actor or an actress saying the words. Like small presses play a major role for marginalized writers, video makers play a major role in film for us. A focused camera eye is powerful.

BK: How did you settle on the title *Under the Feet of Jesus*?

My working title at first was "Migratory." I was an M.F.A. student at U. C. Irvine, and I was surrounded by some very talented writers. One young man pointed out the documents under the feet of Jesus. He said, "My God! That is so captivating. It's so amazing. How could you have imagined that?" I said, "That's what my mother used to do." My mother used to slip all the important papers under the feet of Jesus. She has an altar at home. So I changed it to *Under the Feet of Jesus* and it seemed to work out. I truly believe that if you sit and meditate enough, things will surface that you had no conscious idea about. This is another thing that Márquez really emphasized, trusting the subconscious to work itself out. To a certain extent, the title has various connections with the book, partly serendipity, partly subconscious, strictly not of my own creative duty.

BK: What was your goal in referring to Estrella's mother, Petra, as THE MOTHER? Was that a conscious decision?

It was a very conscious choice on my part because I wanted to show Petra in different dimensions and different roles. When she is with Estrella, she is The Mother. But when she is with Perfecto, she is The Lover. It's one of the things we don't see enough in terms of our own mothers. We only see our mothers as sacred. We don't see them as human beings. The irony is that when Estrella is coming into her own reality, Petra is a lover of this older man. So this is why I called her THE MOTHER. That is adolescence. It is painful. But what I did have in mind was Estrella seeing her one way and Perfecto another. But it was mostly for the dimension of the personality, a contrast between the sacred and the sexual.

BK: Why do you begin, "Had they been heading for the barn all along?" What does this symbol mean to you?

I was reading Erlinda Gonzales-Berry's [critic of Chicana literature] "Rosebud." She had written a passage in which the father prohibits the girls from going into the barn. Any time that something is prohibited due to the nature of being female, one has to think about that. I thought, why would that happen? At first, I thought the obvious is sexuality, the roll in the haystack, and then there's animal intercourse. Also, raw beastly birth. Why should a young girl be prevented from knowing sexuality? The barn is also a rejection of her mother's faith but a reemphasis as well. It's also how incredibly powerful we women can become. No wonder that throughout all these generations, sexuality has been so suppressed in us, that has been derailed, that has been distorted because it is so powerful. Then you are fucking ready to face the world. There is no stopping you. To me, that was her. By the end, the barn gave her that power.

JH: Could you comment on the adolescent relationship between Alejo and Estrella? I sense ambiguity there.

I don't know if it comes out in the book, but I wavered between a romantic love and a friendship between the two. At one point, Alejo really has the hots for her. The first thing he sees is her swimming naked in the canal. But he does not see who she is but what she is. For him, it's a romantic love. For her, she has never met anyone like him, never met anyone who can tell her about things other than the world she has lived. She is not exposed that much to books. I think she is a real wise woman, wiser than I am. She has given reinforced hope about my own power. If I have created a character as powerful as Estrella, then there must be a hope and power in myself to do this. So even she has given me faith. This is all going back to the creative process and the imagination. Once you let the light lead you to realize that you have that power, it's great!

BK: Some characters speak in Spanish. You use much more Spanish than you previously have. What is your goal in doing this?

A few years ago, a southwestern writer, Cormac McCarthy, wrote *All the Pretty Horses*. If I remember correctly, there were whole paragraphs in Spanish. Not one reviewer questioned it, not one reader said, "I wish there was a glossary." But if a Spanish-surnamed writer uses Spanish, it becomes an issue. Readers feel purposefully excluded, like, why are you keeping this from me? Well, I'm sorry. How could I not give integrity to the characters? I only italicize when the character Petra is singing, and those are not her words or my words. That's another song. By using Spanish, did you miss out on the story? I feel out of the loop too when people use French words. I'm trying to do my work as a writer to integrate the meaning within the context of the story so that the meaning is not missed because of not knowing Spanish. There was a question shortly after the novel went into press whether Spanish should be italicized. I said, "Absolutely not." I don't want to call attention to the text. But a lot of non-Spanish speakers who have been reading *Under the Feet of Jesus* feel that there is a minimal frustration in terms of Spanish. They have gotten the context of the story. I'm satisfied. I would never, never jeopardize the voices of these characters. How could I possibly? Fortunately, we have become part of the American text in the nineties, in terms of the literary canon. There are always some anthologies that are part of college text curricula. We are slowly having some bend.

BK: I sense a bit of Faulkner in this work. Was he an influence at all?

When I was thinking of Estrella's story line of the initiation, I thought of Faulkner's "Bear." But only in terms of story line, in terms of the acts of initiation, the tests that have to be done to become an adult. But that is as far as it goes. Faulkner is Faulkner. He is a wonderful writer, and at some point or another, he gave the permission that one could write what one could write, given the possibilities. I'm sure at one point or another, he has influenced me.

JH: In this novel, memory plays a vital role through the use of music. The songs in Spanish are very symbolic in finding hope of a new life in the United States.

Well, I wanted to humanize farmworkers. The only way to oppress a people is by dehumanizing or demonizing them. That way it is easy for them to say such horrible racist remarks like "No mueren. No pasan."—this kind of bullshit that goes on in immigration videos. I wanted to show that people love, that people marry, that people have dreams, that people have children. These are the stories that I wanted to put forth. As for the songs, Professor María Herrera-Sobek has published a wonderful book on the corridos titled *Northward Bound*. Her studies on the corridos give me a better appreciation of our oral tradition, as well as the utter importance of the form as a cultural survival tool. How better to record one's history and life, if not by song? How else can it be done when there are no books? These songs are often sad and lonely.

JH: How is teaching creative writing at Cornell?

It's interesting, because I thought I was going to be at Cornell with up-tight students. I thought, Oh, my God! The problems and everything else. I remember that when I started teaching I wrote to Sandra [Cisneros], who wrote back to me, "Just give them yourself. That is all you can give them." I went there, admitted things that I did not know. I worked on things that I did. Let me tell you that I enjoy my students very much. They are always so excited about engaging in writing. Writing is a gift you give to yourself. So they engage once you say it is O.K. to think about what your heart is feeling. It is O.K. to spend a whole hour experimenting on one word. Let me tell you, man, they are ecstatic! They are very, very happy! When they feel happy, I feel happy. By and large, my students have given me a lot. So it's been a very, very pleasant experience.

BK: It sounds like it's complementary to your own writing.

Yes and no. It's very draining, because you use one level of imaginative powers when you are commenting and criticizing and also when you are rewriting people's work in your head. There are so many things to do in terms of teaching that I don't think that I am going to have time to write. I've been trying to maintain my writing in any way possible. I have slowly resigned myself to work really hard to get as much done as I can. I have two jumps. I am a professor, and I am doing my committee work. But I also have to come home and do my own work.

BK: How do you find time in your busy schedule to write?

If you don't find time for writing, it'll haunt you like a ghost on a revenge mission. But to also sit your ass to the chair, as Richard Rhodes wrote, is the hardest decision to make because it's downright lonely. We arrive in our seats with our sense of insecurities as human beings incapable of capturing the visions in our heads. With our open bleeding hearts, we arrive to make some understanding for ourselves and for the readers. The whole process can be very hurtful, emotionally and spiritually. Writers are often alone.

JH: But doesn't solitude help your writing?

To be alone with your hurt and insecurity is not a good thing, and yet these are companions of writers. Just when I think I'm sinking into hopelessness, I begin to think about the stories of the mujeres out there, their sheer arrogance to survive, their incredible strength to take care of others, and the brutalities that continue to exist, and then I become inspired and I am no longer afraid of confronting and sitting with these companions, like O.K., Lucha Libre, let's get rolling. Some people think that writing is such an easy thing; as if we sit down and it all comes to us. No, we have to wait for the universe to signal the impulse, and we have to be prepared to see it all, both the good and the evil, with our open eyes and be grateful for the opportunity to see inside your soul. To simply sit there and be patient, with absolutely no guarantee that the spirits will whisper in your ear, that's courageousness. I think we writers are some of the bravest people in the world, and because we learn to become fearless through the creative process, we can be dangerously revolutionary. We believe wholeheartedly in the power of the imagination to create the possible, and no one, no one can control that fact. We have breathed new life into social engagement. We are knocking at the door demanding change. It would behoove you to answer because you can't imagine what rage we mujeres have.

JH: What motivates you in organizing academic conferences?

When I go to other conferences, I see what captures my imagination. If I am excited about these things, the first thing I want to do is share it. I meet people. If I see commonalities, I want to put them in a room together. With "Chicana Creativity and Criticism," I was very much interested in the interaction between writers and critics. In *Chicana W(rites)*, I was interested in bringing the dimension of film, because this genre is such a marginalized aspect of artistic creativity. Women are doing phenomenal work! It's almost like the haiku of videomaking. In "U.S. Latina Feminism" at Cornell, nobody had heard of this. This was groundbreaking in bringing everyone together. It was an incredible success. I don't know how many people from universities on the East Coast had driven up to attend. It was wonderful to see people so interested.

JH: Could you talk about *They Came with Their Dogs* [the novel]?

It has so many different facets to it. At first I wanted to write about the colonized imagination—how we have learned to hate ourselves as a people so much that we kill one another, as in gang violence. That is the basic premise. I felt that I had to excavate the history of colonization. The book starts out with an epigram from Miguel Portillo's *The Broken Spear: The Aztec Account of the Conquest of México* and the whole idea of dogs, how the Spaniards have brought in these dogs and trained them to rip flesh. I can unravel the violence that perpetrates it and the ambiance that perpetrates it. I can go back to the sixties. It deals with a lost community divided by freeways. It deals with fragmentations of the self and society. It's a really weird book. Every day that I sit down to write, it's a scary experience for me. It's a hard book. I think it whirled me into a feeling of depression. Because to be writing this book and to be sitting out here where there is no sun five days, it's like Oh, fuck. It's like nothing I've written before. It was the symbol of the dogs that I started excavating. Before you know it, this story has grown into this vast impression of the world situated in a little corner of East L.A., which I am finding really hard to write about.

JH: What has writing fiction given to you as a human being?

In working with the novel, it has given me the ability to explore the world, to create a world. Writing is truly my meditation to the world. It is the way I try to understand a response or an emotion. I try to work it out, the whole process of writing, and I truly believe that it is like a force, like a revelation, that consistently pushes you to come to the meaning of what it is like to be human. I bring the emotions to the surface, bring them on the table. I think this is as important as writing a vision. Sometimes I am such a meager human being that I have no answers. If I did not have writing, I don't know what I would have done. It has really, really given me my prayer to the world. The genre of fiction is an incredible force. It's also very mysterious and mythical. I tell my students to go back to that moment of mystery. You have forgotten what it is like to be children, everything we saw with fascination and excitement and curiosity until we realized that no, things were not that way. But a writer gives that back to you, to get that again, to open up all of your senses. You become a human being who sees clearer and smells stronger, who hears better, who feels with so much more force. So you become much more engaged in life because you feel what writing does to you.

Bibliography

PRIMARY TEXTS

Alvarez, Julia. *Homecoming*. New York: Grove, 1984.

———. *The Housekeeping Book*. Burlington, VT: Alvarez, Macdonald, Schall, 1984.

———. *How the García Girls Lost Their Accents*. Chapel Hill: Algonquin Books, 1991.

———. *In the Time of the Butterflies*. Chapel Hill: Algonquin Books, 1994.

———. *Something to Declare*. Chapel Hill: Algonquin Books, 1998.

———. *¡YO!* Chapel Hill: Algonquin Books, 1997.

Chávez, Denise. *Face of an Angel*. New York: Farrar, Straus & Giroux, 1994.

———. *The Last of the Menu Girls*. Houston: Arte Público Press, 1986.

———. *Loving Pedro Infante*. Farrar, Straus & Giroux. 2000.

Cisneros, Sandra. "Do You Know Me? I Wrote *The House on Mango Street*." *Americas Review* 15.1 (1987): 77–79.

———. "The Genius of Creative Flexibility." The Nation/Leadership: Home Edition Opinion, *Los Angeles Times*. Feb. 22, 1998: 2.

———. "Ghosts and Voices: Writing from Obsession." *Americas Review* 15.1 (1987): 69–73.

———. *The House on Mango Street*. Houston: Arte Público Press, 1984.

———. "Introduction." In *The House on Mango Street*. New York: Alfred A. Knopf, 1994.

———. *Loose Woman*. New York: Vintage Books, 1994.

————. *My Wicked Wicked Ways*. New York: Vintage Books, [1987] 1992.

————. "My Wicked Wicked Ways: The Chicana Writer's Struggle with Good and Evil or *Las Hijas de la Malavida*." Unpublished.

————. "Notes to a Young(er) Writer." *Americas Review* 15.1 (1987): 74–76.

————. *Woman Hollering Creek and Other Stories*. New York: Random House, 1991.

Ferré, Rosario. *El árbol y sus sombras*. México, DF: Fondo de Cultura Económica, 1989.

————. *El coloquio de las perras*. Río Piedras, Puerto Rico: Editorial Cultural, 1990.

————. *Cortázar, el romántico en su observatorio*. San Juan, Puerto Rico: Editorial Cultural, 1990.

————. *Las dos Venecias*. México, DF: Joaquín Mortiz, 1992.

————. *Eccentric Neighborhoods*. New York: Farrar, Straus & Giroux, 1997.

————. *Fabulas de la garza desangrada*. México, DF: Joaquín Mortiz, 1982.

————. *The House on the Lagoon*. New York: Plume, 1996.

————. *Maldito amor*. México, DF: Joaquín Mortiz, 1986.

————. *El medio pollito: Siete cuentos infantiles*. Río Piedras, Puerto Rico: Ediciones Huracán, 1976.

————. *Memorias de Ponce: Autobiografia de Luis A. Ferré Narradas por Rosario Ferré*. San Juan, Puerto Rico: Editorial Cultural, 1996.

————. *Papeles de Pandora*. México, DF: Joaquín Mortiz, 1976.

————. *Sonatinas*. Río Piedras, Puerto Rico: Ediciones Huracán, 1989.

————. *Sweet Diamond Dust*. New York: Ballantine Books, 1988. Translation by *Ferré*.

————. *The Youngest Doll and Other Stories*. Lincoln: University of Nebraska Press, 1991.

————. "Blessings of the Butt." *Body*. Ed. Steve Fiffer and Sharon Fiffer. New York: Avon Books, 1999, 191–98.

García, Cristina. *The Agüero Sisters*. New York: Alfred A. Knopf, 1997.

————. *Dreaming in Cuban*. New York: Ballantine Books, 1992.

————. "Tito's Goodbye." *Iguana Dreams: New Latino Fiction*. Ed. Delia Poey and Virgil Suarez. New York: HarperCollins, 1992, 75–80.

Mohr, Nicholasa. *El Bronx Remembered*. New York: Harper and Row, 1975.

————. *Felita*. New York: Dial, 1979.

————. *Going Home*. New York: Dial Books for Young Readers, 1986.

————. *In My Own Words: Growing Up Inside the Sanctuary of My Imagination*. New York: Simon and Schuster, 1994.

————. *In Nueva York*. New York: Dial, 1977.

————. "Introduction." *Latinas! Women of Achievement*. Ed. Jim Kamp and Diane Telgin. Detroit: Visible Ink Press, 1996.

———. "The Journey toward a Common Ground: Struggle and Identity of Hispanics in the U.S.A." *Americas Review* 18.1 (Spring 1990): 81–85.

———. *A Matter of Pride and Other Stories*. Houston: Arte Público Press, 1997.

———. *Nilda*. New York: Harper and Row, 1973.

———. "Puerto Rican Writers in the United States, Puerto Rican Writers in Puerto Rico: A Separation Beyond Language." *Americas Review* 15.2 (1987): 87–92.

———. *Ritual of Survival: A Woman's Portfolio*. Houston: Arte Público Press, 1985.

Moraga, Cherríe. *Giving Up the Ghost*. Los Angeles: West End Press, 1986.

———. *Heroes and Saints and Other Plays*. Albuquerque: West End Press, 1986.

———. *The Last Generation: Prose and Poetry*. Boston: South End Press, 1993.

———. *Loving in the War Years: Lo que nunca pasó por sus labios*. Boston: South End Press, 1983.

———. *Waiting in the Wings: Portrait of a Queer Motherhood*. Ithaca, NY: Firebrand Books, 1997.

Moraga, Cherríe, and Gloria Anzaldúa, eds. *This Bridge Called My Back: Writings by Radical Women of Color*. New York: Kitchen Table Press; Women of Color Press, 1981.

Moraga, Cherríe, Alma Gómez and Mariana Romo-Carmona. *Cuentos: Stories by Latinas*. New York: Kitchen Table Press; Women of Color Press, 1983.

Ortiz Cofer, Judith. *An Island Like You: Stories of the Barrio*. New York: Orchard Books, 1995.

———. *The Latin Deli*. Athens: University of Georgia Press, 1993.

———. *Latin Women Pray*. Fort Lauderdale: Florida Arts Gazette Press, 1980.

———. *The Line of the Sun: A Novel*. Athens: University of Georgia Press, 1989.

———. *Peregrina*. New York: Riverstone, 1986.

———. *Reaching for the Mainland*. Tempe, AZ: Bilingual Press, 1987.

———. *Silent Dancing: A Partial Remembrance of a Puerto Rican Childhood*. Houston: Arte Público Press, 1990.

———. *Terms of Survival: Poems*. Houston: Arte Público Press, 1987.

———. *The Year of Our Revolution*. Houston: Arte Público Press, 1998.

Santiago, Esmeralda. *Almost a Woman*. New York: Random House, 1999.

———. *América's Dream and El sueño de América*. Trans. Esmeralda Santiago. New York: HarperCollins, 1996.

———. *Las Christmas: Favorite Latino Authors Share Their Holiday Memories*. Co-ed. Joie Davidow. New York: Alfred A. Knopf, 1998.

———. "The Closet." *Home: American Writers Remember Rooms of Their Own*. Ed. Steve Fiffer and Sharon Fiffer. New York: Pantheon/Random House, 1995.

———. "Skin." *Body*. Ed. Steve Fiffer and Sharon Fiffer. New York: Avon Books, 1999, 61–72.

———. *Cuando era puertorriqueña*. Trans. Esmeralda Santiago. New York: Vintage, 1994.

————. "Island of Lost Causes" and "The American Invasion of Macún." Ed. Roberto Santiago. *Boricuas*. New York: Ballantine/Random House, 1995.

————. "Mensaje en el Natalicio de Luis Muñoz Rivera." *Perspectivas sobre Puerto Rico en homenaje a Muñoz Rivera y Muñoz Marín*. San Juan, Puerto Rico: Fundación Luis Muñoz Marín, 1997.

————. *When I Was Puerto Rican*. New York: Random House, 1993.

————. "Why Women Remain Jamona." *Growing Up Puerto Rican*. Ed. Joy L. De Jesus. New York: William Morrow, 1997.

Viramontes, Helena María. "The Jumping Bean." *Chicana (W)rites on Word and Film*. Ed. María Herrera-Sobek and Helena María Viramontes. Berkeley: Third Woman Press, 1995, 101–12.

————. "Miss Clairol." *Chicana Creativity: Charting New Frontiers in American Literature*. Ed. María Herrera-Sobek and Helena María Viramontes. Albuquerque: University of New Mexico Press, 1996 [1987], 164–68.

————. *The Moths and Other Stories*. Houston: Arte Público Press, 1985.

————. "Nopalitos: The Making of Fiction." *Breaking Boundaries: Latina Writing and Critical Readings*. Ed. Asunción Horno-Delgado, Eliana Ortega, Nina M. Scott and Nancy Saporta Sternbach. Amherst: University of Massachusetts Press, 1989, 33–38.

————. "La Ofrenda: Doy mi palabra/I Give My Word." *Las formas de nuestras voces: Chicana and Mexicana Writers in Mexico*. Ed. Claire Joysmith. Berkeley: Third Woman Press, 1995, 99–103.

————. "Requiem for the Poor." *Statement Magazine*. Los Angeles: California State University, Los Angeles, 1976, 12–17.

————. *Under the Feet of Jesus*. New York: Dutton, 1995.

CRITICAL AND GENERAL TEXTS

Acosta-Belen, Edna. "The Literature of the Puerto Rican Minority in the United States." *Bilingual Review/La Revista Bilingue* 5.1–2 (1978): 107–16.

————. "A MELUS Interview: Judith Ortiz Cofer." *MELUS: Journal of the Society for the Study of the Multi-Ethnic Literature of the United States* 18.3 (Fall 1993): 83–97.

Adams, Kate. "North American Silences: History, Identity, and Witness in the Poetry of Gloria Anzaldúa, Cherríe Moraga, and Leslie Marmon Silko." *Listening to Silences: New Essays in Feminist Criticism*. Ed. Elaine Hedges and Shelley Fisher Fishkin. New York: Oxford University Press, 1994, 130–45.

Alarcón, Norma. "Chicana Writers and Critics in a Social Context: Towards a Contemporary Bibliography." *Sexuality of Latinas*. Ed. Norma Alarcón, Ana Castillo and Cherríe Moraga. Berkeley: Third Woman Press, 1993, 169–78.

————. "Interview with Cherrie Moraga." *Third Woman* 3.1–2 (1986): 126–34.

————. "Latina Writers in the United States." *Spanish American Women Writers:*

A Bibliography of Women's Issues. Ed. Diane Marting. Westport, CT: Greenwood Press, 1990, 557–67.

———. "Making Familia from Scratch: Split Subjectivities in the Work of Helena María Viramontes and Cherríe Moraga." *Chicana Creativity and Criticism: New Frontiers in American Literature.* Ed. María Herrera-Sobek and Helena María Viramontes. Albuquerque: University of New Mexico Press, 1996, 220–32.

Alegría, Fernando, and Jorge Ruffinelli, eds. *Paradise Lost or Gained: The Literature of Hispanic Exile.* Houston: Arte Público Press, 1990.

Alvarez Borland, Isabel. "Displacements and Autobiography in Cuban-American Fiction." *World Literature Today* 68.1 (1994): 43–48.

Anderson, Douglas. "Displaced Abjection and States of Grace: Denise Chavez's *The Last of the Menu Girls.*" *American Women Short Story Writers: A Collection of Critical Essays.* Ed. Julie Brown. New York: Garland, 1995, 235–50.

Anzaldúa, Gloria. *Borderlands/La frontera: The New Mestiza.* San Francisco: Spinsters/Aunt Lute, 1987.

Aparicio, Frances, and Susana Chávez-Silverman. *Transculturation: Cultural Representations of Latinidad.* Hanover: Dartmouth Press, 1997.

Arteaga, Alfred. "Heterotextual Reproduction." *Chicano Poetics* (Fall 1996): 61–85.

Behar, Ruth. Introduction. Special Issue: *Bridges to Cuba/Puentes a Cuba. Michigan Quarterly Review* 33.3 (Summer 1994): 399–414.

Binder, Wolfgang, ed. *Partial Autobiographies: Interviews with Twenty Chicano Poets.* Erlangen: Verlag Palm & Enke Erlange, 1985.

Bow, Leslie. "Hole to Whole: Feminine Subversion and Subversion of the Feminine in Cherríe Moraga's *Loving in the War Years.*" *Dispositio* 16.41 (1991): 1–12.

Brady, Mary Pat, and Juanita Heredia. "Coming Home: Interview with Cherríe Moraga." *Mester* 22.2 (1993), 23.1 (1994): 181–96.

Bruce-Novoa, Juan. "Judith Ortiz Cofer's Rituals of Movement." *Americas Review* 19.3–4 (Winter 1991): 88–99.

———. "Ritual in Judith Ortiz Cofer's *The Line of the Sun.*" *Confluencia: Revista Hispanica de Cultura y Literatura* 8.1 (Fall 1992): 61–69.

Calderón, Hector. "At the Crossroads of History, On the Borders of Change: Chicano Literary Studies Past, Present and Future." *Left Politics and the Literary Profession.* Ed. Lennard J. Davis and M. Bella Mirabella. New York: Columbia University Press, 1990, 211–35.

Calderón, Héctor, and José David Saldívar, eds. *Criticism in the Borderlands: Studies in Chicano Literature, Culture, and Ideology.* Durham: Duke University Press, 1992.

Canning, Charlotte. "Contemporary Feminist Theatre." *American Drama.* Ed. Clive Bloom. New York: St. Martin's, 1995, 178–92.

Carter, Nancy Corson. "Claiming the Bittersweet Matrix: Alice Walker, Sandra

Cisneros, and Adrienne Rich." *Critique* 5.4 (Summer 1994): 195–204.

Case, Sue-Ellen. "Seduced and Abandoned: Chicanas and Lesbians in Representation." *Negotiating Performance: Gender, Sexuality, and Theatricality in Latino America.* Ed. Diana Taylor, Juan Villegas, and Tiffany Ana López. Durham: Duke University Press, 1994, 88–101.

Castillo, Debra A. "The Daily Shape of Horses: Denise Chávez and Maxine Hong Kingston." *Dispositio* 16.41 (1991): 29–43.

Castillo-Speed, Lillian, ed. *Latina: Women's Voices from the Borderlands.* New York: Simon and Schuster, 1995.

Chabram, Angie, and Rosalinda Fregoso, eds. "Chicana/o Cultural Representations: Reframing Critical Discourse." Special Issue. *Cultural Studies* 4.3 (1990): 203–12.

De Jesús, Joy L., ed. *Growing Up Puerto Rican.* New York: William Morrow, 1997.

Diaz Quiñones, Arcadio. *La memoria rota.* San Juan, Puerto Rico: Ediciones Huracán, 1993.

Dispositio 16.41 (1991). Special Issue. "Toward a Theory of Latino Literature."

Doyle, Jacqueline. "More Room of Her Own: Sandra Cisneros's *The House on Mango Street.*" *MELUS* 19. 4 (Winter 1994): 5–35.

Dwyer, June. "The Wretched Refuse at the Golden Door: Nicholasa Mohr's 'The English Lesson' and America's Persistent Patronizing of Immigrants." *Proteus* 11.2 (1994 Fall): 45–48.

Eysturoy, Annie. *Daughters of Self-Creation: The Contemporary Chicana Novel.* Albuquerque: University of New Mexico Press, 1996.

Eysturoy, Annie O. "Denise Chávez." *This Is about Vision: Interviews with Southwestern Writers.* Ed. William Balassi, John Crawford, and Annie O. Eysturoy. Albuquerque: University of New Mexico Press, 1990, 157–69.

Fabre, Genevieve. "Liminality, In-Betweenness and Indeterminacy: Notes toward an Anthropological Reading of Judith Cofer's *The Line of the Sun.*" *ACRAA* 18 (1993): 223–32.

Fabre, Genevieve, ed. *European Perspectives on Hispanic Literature of the United States.* Houston: Arte Público Press, 1988.

Fernández, Roberta. "'The Cariboo Cafe': Helena María Viramontes Discourse with Her Social and Cultural Contexts." *Women's Studies* 17.1–2 (1989): 71–85.

Fernández, Roberta, ed. *In Other Words: Literature by Latinas of the United States.* Houston: Arte Público Press, 1994.

Fernández Olmos, Margarite. "Growing Up Puertorriquena: The Feminist Bildungsroman and the Novels of Nicholasa Mohr and Magali Garcia Ramis." *Centro* 2.7 (Winter 1989–90): 56–73.

Flores, Juan. "Back Down These Mean Streets: Introducing Nicholasa Mohr and Louis Reyes Rivera." *Revista Chicano-Riquena* 8.2 (1980): 51–56.

————. *Divided Borders: Essays on Puerto Rican Identity*. Houston: Arte Público Press, 1994.

Franklet, Duane. "Social Language: Bakhtin and Viramontes." *Americas Review* 17.2 (Summer 1989): 110–14.

Ganz, Robin. "Sandra Cisneros: Border Crossings and Beyond." *MELUS* 19.1 (1994): 19–30.

Gómez, Alma, Cherríe Moraga, and Mariana Romo-Carmona, eds. *Cuentos: Stories by Latinas*. New York: Kitchen Table Press, 1983.

Gonzáles-Berry, Erlinda. "Unveiling Athena: Women in the Chicano Novel." *Chicana Critical Issues*. Ed. Norma Alarcón. Berkeley: Third Woman Press, 1993, 33–44.

González-Berry, Erlinda, and Tey Diana Rebolledo. "Growing Up Chicano: Tomás Rivera and Sandra Cisneros." *Americas Review* 13.3–4 (1985): 109–19.

Gray, Lynn. "Interview with Denise Chavez." *Short Story Review* 5.4 (Fall 1988): 2–4.

Gregory, Lucille H. "The Puerto Rican 'Rainbow': Distortions vs. Complexities." *Children's Literature Association Quarterly* 18.1 (Spring 1993): 29–35.

Grobman, Laurie. "The Cultural Past and Artistic Creation in Sandra Cisneros' *The House on Mango Street* and Judith Ortiz Cofer's *Silent Dancing*." *Confluencia* 2.1 (Fall 1995): 42–49.

Gutiérrez-Jones, Leslie S. "Different Voices: The Re-Bildung of the Barrio in Sandra Cisneros' *The House on Mango Street*." *Anxious Power: Reading, Writing, and Ambivalence in Narrative by Women*. Ed. Carol J. Singley and Elizabeth Sweeney. Albany: SUNY Press, 1993.

Heard, Martha E. "The Theatre of Denise Chavez: Interior Landscapes with 'sabornuevomexicano.'" *Americas Review* 16.2 (Summer 1988): 83–91.

Heredia, Juanita. "Down These City Streets: Exploring Urban Space in *El Bronx Remembered* and *The House on Mango Street*." *Mester* 22.2 (Fall 1993), 23.1 (Spring 1994): 93–105.

Heredia, Juanita, and Silvia Pellarolo. "East of Downtown and Beyond: Interview with Helena María Viramontes." *Mester* 22.2 (Fall 1993), 23.1 (Spring 1994): 165–80.

Herrera, Andrea O'Reilly. "'Chambers of Consciousness': Sandra Cisneros and the Development of the Self in the BIG House on Mango Street." *Bucknell Review* 39.1 (1995): 191–204.

Herrera-Sobek, María, and Helena María Viramontes. *Chicana Creativity: Charting New Frontiers in American Literature*. Houston: Arte Público Press, 1987.

————. *Chicana (W)rites on Word and Film*. Berkeley: Third Woman Press, 1995.

Horno-Delgado, Asunción, Eliana Ortega, Nina M. Scott, and Nancy Saporta Sternbach, eds. *Breaking Boundaries: Latina Writing and Critical Readings*. Amherst: University of Massachusetts Press, 1989.

Jay, Julia de Foor. "(Re)claiming the Race of the Mother: Cherríe Moraga's *Shadow of a Man, Giving Up the Ghost*, and *Heroes and Saints*." Ed. Elizabeth Brown-Guillory. *Women of Color: Mother-Daughter Relationships in 20th-Century Literature.* Austin: University of Texas Press, 1996, 95–116.

Kanellos, Nicolás, ed. *Hispanic Literary Companion.* Detroit: Visible Ink Press, 1997.

———. *Short Fiction by Hispanic Writers of the United States.* Houston: Arte Público Press, 1993.

Klein, Dianne. "Coming of Age in Novels by Rudolfo Anaya and Sandra Cisneros." *English Journal* 81.5 (Sept. 1992): 21–26.

Kolmar, Wendy K. "'Dialectics of Connectedness': Supernatural Elements in Novels by Bambara, Cisneros, Grahn, and Erdrich." *Haunting the House of Fiction: Feminist Perspectives on Ghost Stories by American Women.* Ed. Lynette Carpenter and Wendy K. Kolmar. Knoxville: University of Tennessee Press, 1991, 236–49.

Lawless, Cecelia. "Helena Maria Viramontes' Homing Devices in *Under the Feet of Jesus*." *Homemaking: Women Writers and the Politics and Poetics of Home.* Ed. Catherine Wiley and Fiona R. Barnes. New York: Garland, 1996, 361–82.

López, Iraida H. ". . . And There Is Only My Imagination Where Our History Should Be: An Interview with Cristina García." Special Issue: *Bridges to Cuba/Puentes a Cuba. Michigan Quarterly Review* 33.3 (Summer 1994): 604–17.

Luis, William. *Dance between Two Cultures: Latino Caribbean Literature Written in the United States.* Nashville: Vanderbilt University Press, 1997.

Lynn, Dennis, and Daly Heyck, eds. *Barrios and Borderlands.* New York: Routledge, 1994.

McCracken, Ellen. "Latina Narrative and Politics of Signification: Articulation, Antagonism, and Populist Rupture." *Critica* 2.2 (Fall 1990): 202–7.

Martín-Rodríguez, Manuel M. "'The Book of 'Mango Street': Escritura y liberación en la obra de Sandra Cisneros." *Mujer y literatura mexicana y chicana: Culturas en contacto.* Ed. Aralia López González, Amelia Malagamba, and Elena Urrutia. Tijuana: El Colegio de México, El Colegio de la Frontera Norte, 1990, 249–54.

Miller, John. "The Concept of Puerto Rico as Paradise Island in the Works of Two Puerto Rican Authors on the Mainland: Nicolasa Mohr and Edward Rivera." *Torre de Papel* 3.2 (Summer 1993): 57–64.

Miller, John C. "The Emigrant and New York City: A Consideration of Four Puerto Rican Writers." *MELUS* 5.3 (1978): 82–99.

———. "Nicholasa Mohr: Neorican Writings in Progress: 'A View of the Other Culture.'" *Revista/Review Interamericana* 9 (1979): 543–54.

Milligan, Bryce, Mary Guerrero Milligan, and Angela de Hoyos. *Daughters of the Fifth Sun: A Collection of Latina Fiction and Poetry.* New York: Riverhead Books, 1995.

Mitchell, David T. "National Families and Familial Nations: Communista Americans in Cristina Garcia's *Dreaming in Cuban.*" *Tulsa Studies* 15.1 (Spring 1996): 51–60.

Natov, Roni, and DeLuca, Geraldine. "An Interview with Nicholasa Mohr." *The Lion and the Unicorn* 11.1 (Apr. 1987): 116–21.

Norton, Jody. "History, Rememory, Transformation: Actualizing Literary Value." *Centennial Review* 38.3 (Fall 1994): 589–602.

Ocasio, Rafael. "The Infinite Variety of the Puerto Rican Reality: An Interview with Judith Ortiz Cofer." *Callaloo: A Journal of African-American and African Arts and Letters* 17.3 (Summer 1994): 730–42.

———. "Puerto Rican Literature in Georgia? An Interview with Judith Ortiz Cofer." *Kenyon Review* 14.4 (Fall 1992): 43–50.

Ocasio, Rafael, and Rita Ganey. "Speaking in Puerto Rican: An Interview with Judith Ortiz Cofer." *Bilingual Review/Revista Bilingue* 17.2 (May–Aug. 1992): 143–46.

Olivares, Julian. "Sandra Cisneros' *The House on Mango Street*, and the Poetics of Space." *Americas Review* 15.3–4 (Fall-Winter 1987): 160–70.

Ortega, Eliana. "Desde la entraña del monstruo: Voces hispanas en EEUU." *La sartén por el mango.* Ed. Patricia Elena González and Eliana Ortega. Río Piedras, Puerto Rico: Editorial Huracán, 1985.

Ortega, Eliana, and Nancy Saporta-Sternbach. "At the Threshold of the Unnamed: Latina Literary Discourse in the Eighties." *Breaking Boundaries: Latina Writing and Critical Readings.* Ed. Asunción Horno-Delgado, Eliana Ortega, Nina M. Scott and Nancy Saporta Sternbach. Amherst: University of Massachussetts Press, 1989, 2–23.

Ortiz-Marquez, Maribel. "From Third World Politics to First World Practices: Contemporary Latina Writers in the United States." *Interventions: Feminist Dialogues on Third World Women's Literature and Film.* Ed. Bishnupriya Ghosh, Brinda Bose, and Chandra Talpad Mohanty. New York: Garland, 1997, 227–44.

Passman, Kristina M. "Demeter, Kore and the Birth of the Self: The Quest for Identity in the Poetry of Alma Villanueva, Pat Mora, and Cherríe Moraga." *Monographic Review* 6 (1990): 323–42. Pavletich, JoAnn, and Margot Gayle Backus. "With His Pistol in Her Hand: Rearticulating Corrido Narrative in Helena María Viramontes' 'Neighbors.'" *Cultural Critique* 27 (Spring 1994): 127–52.

Peña, Terri de la. "Spoken Words." *Off Our Backs* 24.6 (June 1994): 10–11.

Pérez Firmat, Gustavo. *Life on the Hyphen: The Cuban American Way.* Austin: University of Texas Press, 1994.

Piedra, Jose. "His and Her Panics." *Dispositio* 16.41 (1991): 71–93.

Poey, Delia, and Virgil Suárez, eds. *Iguana Dreams: New Latino Fiction.* New York: HarperPerennial, 1992.

————. *Little Havana Blues: An Anthology of Cuban-American Literature.* Houston: Arte Público Press, 1996.

Quintana, Alvina E. *Home Girls: Chicana Literary Voices.* Philadelphia: Temple University Press, 1996.

————. "Politics, Representation and the Emergence of a Chicana Aesthetic." *Cultural Studies* 4.3 (1990): 257–63.

Rebolledo, Tey Diana. *Women Singing in the Snow: A Cultural Analysis of Chicana Literature.* Tucson: University of Arizona Press, 1995.

Rebolledo, Tey Diana, and Eliana S. Rivero, eds. *Infinite Divisions: An Anthology of Chicana Literature.* Tucson: University of Arizona Press, 1993.

Rivero, Eliana. "From Immigrants to Ethnics: Cuban Women Writers in the U.S." *Breaking Boundaries: Latina Writing and Critical Readings.* Ed. Asunción Horno-Delgado, Eliana Ortega, Nina M. Scott and Nancy Saporta Sternbach. Amherst: University of Massachussetts Press, 1989, 189–200.

————. "Frontisleña, Border Islander." Special Issue: *Bridges to Cuba/Puentes a Cuba. Michigan Quarterly Review* 33.3 (Fall 1994): 669–74.

————. "The 'Other's Others': Chicana Identity and Its Textual Expressions." *Encountering the Other(s): Studies in Literature, History, and Culture.* Ed. Gisela Brinker. Albany: SUNY Press, 1995, 239–60.

Rodríguez Aranda, Pilar E. "On the Solitary Fate of Being Mexican, Female, Wicked and Thirty-three: An Interview with Writer Sandra Cisneros." *Americas Review* 18.1 (1990): 64–80.

Rodriguez-Luis, Julio. "De Puerto Rico a Nueva York: Protagonistas femeninas en busca de un espacio propio." *La Torre* 7.27–28 (2) (July-Dec. 1993): 577–94.

Rodriguez Vecchini, Hugo. "Cuando Esmeralda 'era' puertorriquena: Autobiografía etnográfica y autobiografía neopicaresca." *Nomada* 1 (April 1995): 145–60.

Romero, Lora. "'When Something Goes Queer': Familiarity, Formalism, and Minority Intellectuals in the 1980s." *Yale Journal of Criticism* 6.1 (Spring 1993): 121–42.

Rosaldo, Renato. "Fables of the Fallen Guy." *Criticism in the Borderlands: Studies in Chicano Literature, Culture, and Ideology.* Ed. Héctor Calderón and José David Saldívar. Durham: Duke University Press, 1991, 84–93.

Rosario-Sievert, Heather. "Conversation with Julia Alvarez." *Review: Latin American Literature and Arts* 54 (Spring 1997): 31–37.

Rosenberg, Lou. "The House of Difference: Gender, Culture, and the Subject-in-Process on the American Stage." *Critical Essays: Gay and Lesbian Writers of Color.* Ed. Emmanuel S. Nelson. New York: Haworth, 1993, 97–110.

Saldívar, José David. *Border Matters.* Berkeley: University of California Press, 1997.

————. "Frontera Crossings: Sites of Cultural Contestation." *Mester* 22.2 (Fall 1993), 23.1 (Spring 1994): 81–91.

Saldívar, Ramón. *Chicano Narrative: The Dialectics of Difference*. Madison: University of Wisconsin Press, 1990, 171–99.

Saldívar-Hull, Sonia. "Political Identities in Contemporary Chicana Literature: Helena María Viramontes's Visions of the U.S. Third World." *"Writing" Nation and "Writing" Region in America*. Ed. Theo D'Haen and Hans Bertens. Amsterdam: VU, 1996, 156–65.

Santiago, Roberta, ed. *Boricuas: Influential Puerto Rican Writing*. New York: Ballantine, 1995.

Stavans, Ilan. *The Hispanic Condition: Reflections on Culture and Identity in America*. New York: HarperCollins, 1995.

Sternbach, Nancy Saporta. "'A Deep Racial Memory of Love': The Chicana Feminism of Cherríe Moraga." Ed. Asunción Horno-Delgado, Eliana Ortega, Nina Scott, and Nancy Saporta Sternbach. *Breaking Boundaries: Latina Writing and Critical Readings*. Amherst: University of Massachusetts Press, 1989, 48–61.

Stockton, Sharon. "Rereading the Maternal Body: Viramontes' 'The Moths' and the Construction of the New Chicana." *Americas Review* 22.1–2 (Spring-Summer 1994): 212–29.

Thomson, Jeff. "'What Is Called Heaven: 'Identity in Sandra Cisneros' *Woman Hollering Creek*." *Studies in Short Fiction* 31.3 (Summer 1994): 415–24.

Trujillo, Carla. *Living Chicana Theory*. Berkeley: Third Woman Press, 1998.

Trujillo, Carla, ed. *Chicana Lesbians: The Girls Our Mother Warned Us About*. Berkeley: Third Woman Press, 1991.

Turner, Faye. *Puerto Rican Writers at Home in the USA: An Anthology*. Seattle: Open Hand, 1991.

Umpierre, Luz Maria. "Interview with Cherríe Moraga." *Americas Review* 14.2 (Summer 1986): 54–67.

———."Sexualidad y metapoesia: Cuatro poemas de Julia Alvarez." *Americas Review* 17.1 (Spring 1989): 108–14.

Valdes, María Elena de. "The Critical Reception of Sandra Cisneros' *The House on Mango Street*." *Gender, Self, and Society*. Ed. Renate von Bardeleben. New York: Lang, 1990, 287–300.

———. "In Search of Identity in Cisneros' *The House on Mango Street*." *Canadian Review of American Studies* 23.1 (1992): 55–72.

Vorda, Allan. "A Fish Swims in My Lung: An Interview with Cristina García." *Face to Face: Interviews with Contemporary Novelists*. Houston: Rice University Press, 1993, 61–76.

Ward, Skye. "Cherríe Moraga." *Contemporary Lesbian Writers of the United States: A Bio-Bibliographical Critical Sourcebook*. Ed. Sandra Pollack, Denise Knight, and Tucker Farley. Westport, CT: Greenwood, 1993, 379–83.

Wyatt, Jean. "On Not Being La Malinche: Border Negotiations of Gender in

Sandra Cisneros's 'Never Marry a Mexican' and 'Woman Hollering Creek.'"
Tulsa Studies 14.2 (Fall 1995): 243–71.

Yarbro-Bejarano, Yvonne. "Cherríe Moraga's *Giving Up the Ghost*: The Representation of Female Desire." *Third Woman* 3.1–2 (1986): 113–20.

———. "Chicana Literature from a Chicana Feminist Perspective." *Chicana Creativity and Criticism: Charting New Frontiers in American Literature*. Ed. María Herrera-Sobek and Helena María Viramontes. Houston: Arte Público Press, 1987, 139–45.